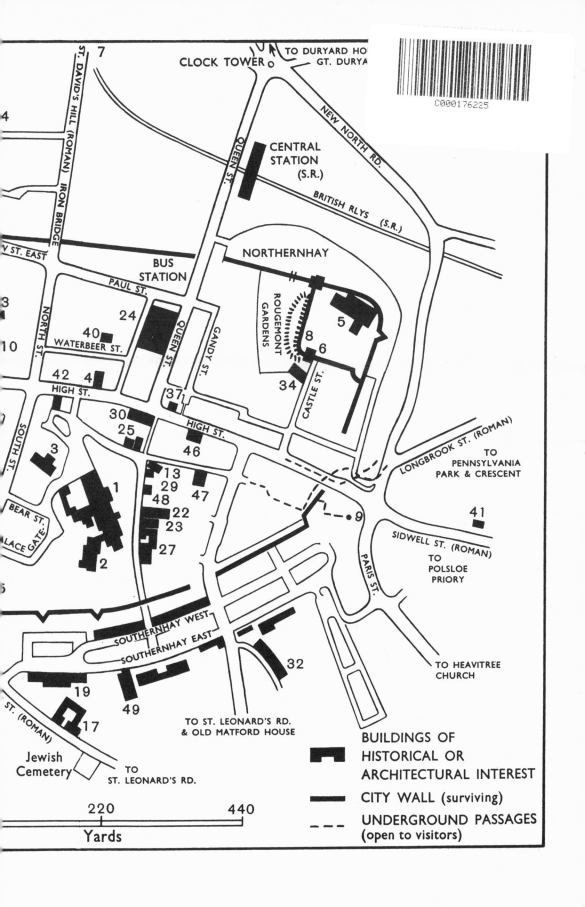

CLOCK TOWER

TO DURYARD HO
GT. DURYA

7

ST. DAVID'S HILL (ROMAN)
IRON BRIDGE

NEW NORTH RD.

CENTRAL
STATION
(S.R.)

QUEEN ST.

BRITISH RLYS (S.R.)

NORTHERNHAY

4

V ST. EAST

BUS
STATION

PAUL ST.

ROUGEMONT
GARDENS

5

3

NORTH ST.

24

40

WATERBEER ST.

QUEEN ST.

GANDY ST.

8

6

10

34

CASTLE ST.

42 4

HIGH ST.

37

30

25

HIGH ST.

46

LONGBROOK ST. (ROMAN)

TO
PENNSYLVANIA
PARK & CRESCENT

SOUTH ST.

3

13
29
48

1

47

22
23

41

27

SIDWELL ST. (ROMAN)
TO
POLSLOE
PRIORY

BEAR ST.

LACE GATE

2

9

PARIS ST.

SOUTHERNHAY WEST

SOUTHERNHAY EAST

32

TO HEAVITREE
CHURCH

19

49

17

ST. (ROMAN)

Jewish
Cemetery

TO
ST. LEONARD'S RD.

TO ST. LEONARD'S RD.
& OLD MATFORD HOUSE

BUILDINGS OF
HISTORICAL OR
ARCHITECTURAL INTEREST

CITY WALL (surviving)

UNDERGROUND PASSAGES
(open to visitors)

220   440

Yards

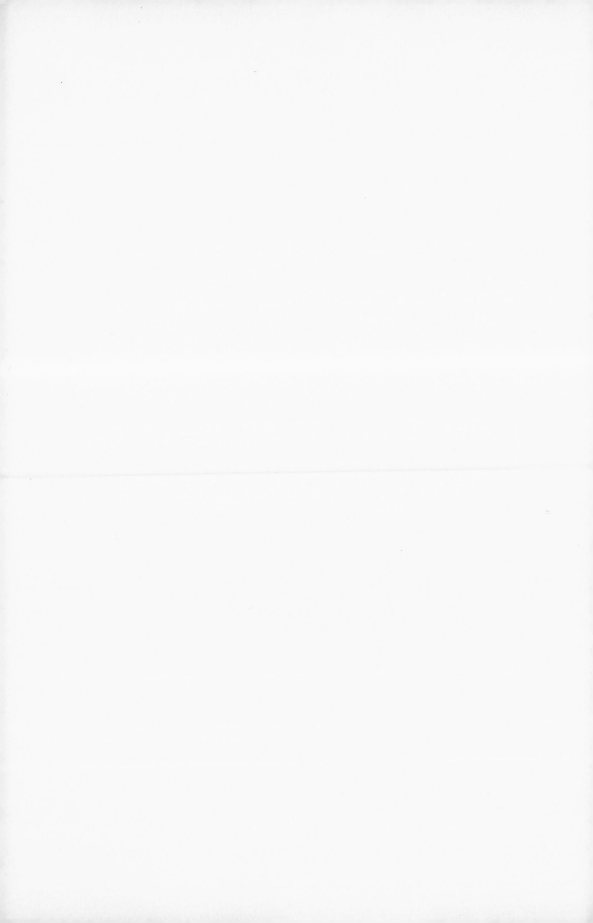

TWO THOUSAND YEARS IN EXETER

Pre-war Exeter showing narrow South Street at the bottom of the photograph, Bedford Circus at the top, St Mary Major church next to the Cathedral's west front, and the cathedral's Norman towers and long Gothic nave.

TWO THOUSAND YEARS IN EXETER

W. G. Hoskins

edited & updated by
Hazel Harvey

 Phillimore

First published 1960
Second impression 1963, reprinted 1969, 1974 and 1979
This revised and updated edition published 2004
by
PHILLIMORE & CO. LTD
Shopwyke Manor Barn, Chichester, West Sussex, England

ISBN 1 86077 303 6

Printed and bound in Great Britain by
ANTONY ROWE
Chippenham, Wiltshire

Contents

List of Illustrations

Preface to the First Edition

There is no adequate history of Exeter and to write one would be a life-work and fill two or three substantial volumes. Since the scale of the present book is relatively small, though no doubt quite sufficient for the general reader, a great deal of Exeter history has necessarily been left out. In this book I have concentrated upon the social history, on people and their doings, and on the kind of buildings and environment which they once enjoyed. Much of the material in this book is new, based upon researches over several years in the city archives and in the Public Record Office.

Once more Mrs Margaret Gray has laboured at the typescript of the book and eased the path of authorship. But I owe most to my wife for producing the domestic conditions in which continuous writing is possible, almost a luxury in these hard-pressed times.

I was born in Exeter, and my father before me, and his father before that. My great-grandfather came to the city as the son of a failing farmer in the bad years of the 1820s, so we have been here a long time. As a native I have been critical of much that is done now in the name of progress (whatever that vague word may mean) but that is the privilege of belonging to the family. One can be critical in ways that would ill become a stranger. Like most Exonians I do not like to hear my native city criticised, but I am ready to do it myself if the occasion demands it. Paradise itself can be no better than Exeter on a summer morning; but even Paradise no doubt has some small faults.

Acknowledgements

In preparing the book I have had some valuable help. Mr Paley, of the city reference library, has been of the greatest possible assistance in answering particular queries, thereby saving me much time; while Mr McKinley, formerly of the city muniment room, was also unfailingly helpful in producing information from the records in his care. For information about some of the old buildings in the city, and on some of its recent social history, I owe much to Mr A.W. Everett, an Exonian with an unrivalled knowledge of the topography of the old city.

I have also consulted the city surveyor (Mr John Brierley) and the city planning officer (Mr Harold Gayton) on many points. They have given me every assistance in their power, for which I am most grateful. Neither they nor anyone else, however, must be held responsible for any views expressed in this book. The historian must make up his own mind on controversial questions in the last resort, and I alone am responsible for what is said in these pages.

W.G. HOSKINS

October 1960

Introduction to the Revised Edition

W.G. Hoskins' *Two Thousand Years in Exeter* has become the definitive history of the city by its most loyal son. It is a privilege to have been invited to update it some forty years after it first appeared. There have been major archaeological discoveries shedding light on the city's early years, although Hoskins was amazingly prescient about what might be found. Tangible evidence now allows the Roman military presence and the early years of Christian practice to be included in Exeter's history.

Exeter is regularly assessed as having a high quality of life. Hoskins would have agreed. After he retired from university teaching and returned to Exeter in 1968, he frequently headed letters to his friends 'From the Elysian Fields' or 'The Shores of Paradise'.

Some information included in the first edition has now been omitted or modified in the light of later developments, but generally I have been reluctant to make changes to Hoskins' authoritative text.

Acknowledgements

W.G. Hoskins' daughter Susan Hewitt and her husband Colin encouraged the production of this revised edition and made many useful suggestions. Colin Hewitt supplied the paragraphs in Chapter Eleven on developments in public transport since 1960. I am grateful for advice from Stuart Blaylock, Richard Parker, Peter Weddell and Mark Stoyle on topographical matters, John Yonge on maps, and Ian Maxted of the Westcountry Studies Library and David Adcock of Exeter City Council on illustrations. Peter Thomas was particularly helpful in supplying historic photos from the Isca Collection. My son Francis helped put the new text on disk and my husband David revised the index as well as helping in many other ways.

I am particularly grateful to all those who supplied illustrations so willingly, rightly believing that it was a privilege to help reissue this classic book. I am indebted to *Current Archaeology* (illustration 3); Devon & Cornwall Constabulary (86); Exeter Archaeology (4-8); Exeter City Council (14, 15, 23, 24, 29, 49); Steve Hall, editor of the *Express and Echo* (85, 91); Deryck Laming (34, 39, 43, 45, 52, 61, 62, 83); George and Pauline Smith (13); Peter Thomas, The Isca Collection (frontispiece, 18, 30-3, 35, 37, 46-8, 50, 54, 57, 59, 63-6, 69-72, 74-82, 87-9, 92); University of Exeter (99); and the Westcountry Studies Library (12, 25, 26, 38, 41, 42, 53, 56, 58, 60, 68). Maps 2, 9, 11, 16 and 20 are from C.G. Henderson's chapter on Exeter in the *Historical Atlas of South-West England* (ed. R. Kain and W. Ravenhill, 1999); Colin and Susan Hewitt provided photos 17, 21, 27, 28, 55, 90, 93-8, 100 and 101. Photos 10, 19, 28 and 36 are by Hazel Harvey.

HAZEL HARVEY

June 2004

CHAPTER ONE

Beginnings: Caerwysc and Isca

The Antiquity of Exeter

HOW OLD IS EXETER as an inhabited place, and where did it originally
start? Is it possible to answer these questions? Everybody knows that Exeter
was a Roman town, but was there any settlement of people here when the
Romans arrived in the South West in the year 49—more than nineteen
hundred years ago?

There is good reason to believe that the site of Exeter, or part of it,
was occupied some considerable time before the Romans appeared on the
scene. This takes us back to a time well before written records, and we
depend therefore on certain material evidence for our scanty knowledge of
this distant time. This material evidence is mainly that of coins which have
been found within the city during various kinds of excavations in the past
200 years; and there is also the evidence of ancient tradition.

Let us take the coins first. In the year 1810, a considerable number
of Hellenistic coins—that is, coins of Greek types from the eastern
Mediterranean struck after the death of Alexander—were found in Broadgate
while workmen were digging at a depth of twenty feet. These coins, the
largest discovery of their kind yet made in this country, could be dated
as belonging to the third, second, and first centuries before Christ. They
suggested some sort of trade at Exeter with the Mediterranean countries
some time between, say, 250 B.C. and the birth of Christ.

This discovery was so remarkable and unexpected that many scholars
refused to believe the evidence. Two distinguished numismatists in 1907,
examining them again, decided that the coins had been planted on the site
in order to cause confusion, or that some private collection had been lost
there. In either event, they decided that the coins were not evidence for the
existence of a trading settlement on the site of Exeter at that early date.

Since they wrote, however, two things have happened to alter the
picture. In the first place, other Hellenistic coins have been found in Exeter
and, secondly, many more have been found at various places along the
south coast of England—for example, at Penzance, at Mount Batten (now
part of Plymouth), and near Poole Harbour in Dorset. We must, therefore,
accept the conclusion that there was considerable trading between the
Mediterranean countries and southern Britain a century or two before the
birth of Christ, and that Exeter (under some other name) was one of the
places engaged in this trade.

Roughly speaking, then, we may say that there were people living in Exeter about 200 years or more before the Romans came, and that Exeter as an inhabited place is about 2,100 years old. It may be somewhat older than this, but no evidence for an earlier date has yet come to light within the city. Excavations in 2003 on the site of the new Crown Courts, however, unearthed traces of Iron-Age occupation—pottery and ditches—on the bank of the Larkbeare stream which led down to the Exe.

Nor do we know what the earliest traders dealt in which would interest Mediterranean countries. It was not likely to be tin—not in Exeter at least, as there is no evidence whatsoever of tin being worked on Dartmoor in prehistoric times. It was more likely to have been cattle and hides, for which Exeter may even then have been the chief market of the whole region. We know that Cornish tin was being exported as early as the fourth century B.C. Continental merchants fetched it possibly from St Michael's Mount, carried it by ship to the west coast of France, and so overland to the mouth of the Rhone and the markets of the Mediterranean countries. It is most likely that the same thing happened at Exeter with cattle, hides, and leather, except that the Continental merchants came in all probability from immediately across the Channel, from such places as Rouen in Normandy, the shortest sea-crossing. It seems very likely then that the processing and marketing of hides and skins, which is still a major undertaking on the Marsh Barton Industrial Estate, is the oldest industry in the city, going back two thousand years.

What else can we say about this early Exeter? One thing is that the High Street is the oldest thoroughfare in the city. It began as an ancient ridgeway some time in the Iron Age, if not earlier, again some two or three

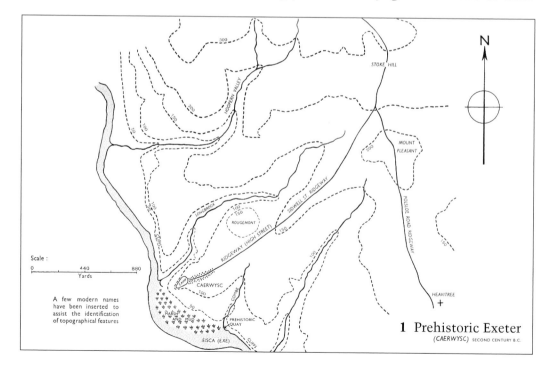

Scale :

0   440   880
         Yards

A few modern names have been inserted to assist the identification of topographical features

1 Prehistoric Exeter
(CAERWYSC) SECOND CENTURY B.C.

centuries before Christ. These ridgeways—roads which run along the back of prominent ridges in order to avoid marshy ground and river crossings as far as possible—are among the oldest roads we have. At Exeter, the ridgeway came down over Stoke Hill (from where we do not yet know). At the top of Old Tiverton Road, where the roundabout now is, it forked. One trackway ran along the top of the conspicuous ridge of Mount Pleasant and so along Polsloe Road (all this line lies on a high ridge to those who keep their eyes open), ending somewhere near Heavitree Church or perhaps going down to the river bank.

The main trackway, however, continued straight down Old Tiverton Road, down what is now Sidwell Street, and so into High Street. This must have been the main route of those early traders. It is significant that the biggest finds of ancient coins were made within a few yards of the High Street.

The earliest inhabitants of Exeter probably lived in the area between Fore Street and Bartholomew Street, in what was hardly more than a native village, despite its widespread trading activities. Exeter has been so much built over in the past two thousand years that it is very difficult to see its original topography—its steep hills, its deep-sided valleys, and its ridges and spurs. But if we think away, so to speak, the modern houses and streets and levels, we find that the ridge along which the High Street ran ended in a spur overlooking the river. The tip of this spur is what is now the disused churchyard of Allhallows-on-the-Walls, ending at the turn in the city walls known as the Snail Tower. On this spur the British had an earthwork—a hill-fortress—of the same type as those we see on the hill-tops of Hembury or Woodbury, though not so grand or formidable. This was their fortress in times of emergency. It seems probable that the earliest inhabitants lived in huts on the leeward side of this spur, on ground sloping gently down to the riverside. Centuries later, this part of Exeter was still known as Britayne (before its name was changed to Bartholomew Street) for it preserved the memory of the time when the ancient British lived there.

The people who lived in Exeter before the Romans came were Celtic. They belonged to a tribe known as the Dumnonii, whose territory covered the whole of South-Western England from Land's End right up to the Parrett Valley in West Somerset. It is possible that Exeter was their tribal capital even before the coming of the Romans, but certainly it became so immediately under Roman rule.

The early inhabitants of Exeter could hardly have numbered more than a few hundreds, about the size of a large village today. The richer among them were traders but most of them were farmers and fishermen. The Exe in those early days teemed with salmon, perhaps as thickly as the rivers of British Columbia today. At any rate, the word Exe derives from a British word *Eisca*, meaning 'a river abounding in fish', and these fish were beyond doubt salmon.

Fishermen must have been a considerable class in the town population. Then there were the farmers, cultivating small plots of ground around the settlement, most probably the level ground now called St Sidwell's, and perhaps raising cattle on the hill slopes to the north and in the marshes near the river in summer. All trace of these ancient farms has disappeared long ago, with the building-up of the city.

The Site of Exeter

There were many good reasons why a village and a trading settlement should have grown up where Exeter stands today. Here a long ridge of dry ground approaches the river, ending in a spur. This ridge formed a small plateau just about 100 feet above the river level, and on this plateau the city later grew. Not only was the plateau well above the river, but it consisted of gravel soils, lying on top of harder rocks. So it not only gave dry soils for building, which were particularly important when the buildings consisted of timber-frame huts with mud walls, but also an unlimited supply of fresh water not far below the surface. Without water no inhabited place could survive for three days; but Exeter has always had an abundance of water from springs and shallow wells sunk through the gravel to the rock below. Hooker, the first historian of Exeter, writing 400 years ago, puts it like this:

> The situation of this city is very pleasant and agreeable, being set upon a little hill among many hills, for the whole country round about is mountainous and full of hills. It slopes towards the south and west parts in such a way that be the streets never so foul or filthy yet with a shower of rain they are cleansed and made sweet. And although the hills are commonly dry yet nature is so beneficial to this little hill that it is in every quarter full of water-springs, and by that means the whole city is thoroughly supplied with wells and tyepitts* to the great benefit and commodity of the city.

In former times, the great majority of houses, especially in the main streets of Exeter, had their own wells. These were fourteen feet down, and at that level they contained four to six feet of fresh water. Practically all these wells have been filled in and would be very difficult to find today, but one was found in 1933 in the Cathedral Close. It may still be seen in the basement of the Well House pub. It is said to be Roman.

Not only did the first inhabitants of Exeter enjoy a high, dry site with an unlimited supply of fresh water for all purposes, but they picked a site which was liberally endowed by nature with all the things necessary for existence. The river produced fish in abundance; corn came from the fertile red lands just outside to the east; and from the pastoral hills to the west came a plentiful supply of meat. All through its history travellers have remarked upon the abundant supplies of meat and fish to be found in Exeter. From the wooded hills to the north of the village came timber for building and fuel for winter fires.

But early Exeter was more than an ordinary British village. It had some overseas trade and here the river was the important factor. At Exeter the wide river suddenly narrowed, just as it does at Topsham today. It was probably the first place at which the Exe could be crossed by means of a

---

* A tyepitt was a deep well.

ford at low tide, and later on it became the first point at which a bridge could be built. It was not until towards the end of the 18th century that another bridge was built below Exeter, at Countess Weir. Furthermore, Exeter stood at the tidal limit of navigation for ships. There is no doubt that the overseas traders who visited Exeter in prehistoric times unloaded their ships at the point where the Custom House now stands. At this point the red sandstone made a hard bench on which traders could congregate, for most of the estuary-banks right down to the sea must have been soft mud under natural conditions, and were flanked by wide marshes. At Exeter there was a good landing-place, and a landing-place moreover at a break in the cliffs which front the river for a considerable distance above and below the city. At Mount Dinham the cliff wall is about seventy feet high, and along the Quay, below Colleton Crescent, it is about fifty feet.

Just where the Custom House stands today was a break in the cliff wall. The observant visitor can still see this natural feature. Not only that, but a stream, which rose in a spring where the cathedral now stands, flowed down a valley (now filled up and called Coombe Street) and entered the river near the present Quay. This meant that goods landed on the natural quay formed by a ledge of red sandstone could be carried into the city without climbing a steep hill, by simply following the little stream upwards from the river-bank until the level plateau was reached.

Again, the site of Exeter lay some ten miles up river from its mouth and this was important when invaders were most likely to come by sea and to attack coastal settlements. At Exeter one was safe from such attacks, or at least there was ample warning of strange ships coming into the estuary. From the volcanic hill we call Rougemont one could look right down to the mouth of the shining estuary and a strange fleet could be spotted hours before it could attack. For all these reasons Exeter made a good trading-place, and above all, of course, it had something to sell—the products of a rich and varied countryside. And so the stage was set for the village to grow into a town, and later still into a rich medieval city, on its hilltop in the far West of England.

The Coming of the Romans

The ancient British name for Exeter seems to have been Caerwysc, meaning 'the fortified town on the Exe', but an even older name occurs in the tradition of a siege by the Roman general Vespasian in the year 49. The tradition tells us that there was already a settlement here when Vespasian was sent westwards, and so supplements the evidence of the Hellenistic coins. At the time of this siege Exeter is said to have been called by the rather formidable name of Caer-pen-huel-goit, which means 'the fortified town on the hill near the high or great wood'.

Such long descriptive place-names are a characteristic of Wales to this day, and it is quite likely that Exeter had some such ancient names as this in prehistoric times. 'The fortified town on the hill' aptly describes the first site of Exeter, with its earthwork on the end of the ridge or hill. 'The high or great wood' probably refers to the wooded hills to the north

of the city, what we now call Stoke Hill and Pennsylvania, which would
have been densely wooded in prehistoric times. Stoke Woods today are a
remnant of this great wood of two thousand and more years ago.

The tradition of a siege by Vespasian has generally been discredited by
modern historians, mainly on the ground that it appears in the writings of
a chronicler (Geoffrey of Monmouth) who is known to be very inaccurate,
if no worse. He tells us that Vespasian was sent down by the Emperor
Claudius to subdue South-West Britain, and that he besieged Exeter for
eight days without success. A British king then arrived from the east with
an army and fought with Vespasian. Despite great losses on both sides
neither got the victory. The next morning, by the mediation of the British
queen, the two leaders made peace.

Archaeological excavations in the 1970s found evidence to support this
medieval tradition, in the form of extensive remains of a Roman military
fortress built on the hill-top where Exeter subsequently developed as a
city. In 1970 a sunken car-park was planned for the Cathedral Green. The
Victorian church of St Mary Major near the west front of the cathedral
was demolished to make way for it. In Chapter Two we shall see that this
revealed traces of the Anglo-Saxon abbey and early Christian cemeteries, but
here we must list the important Roman discoveries, which transformed our
understanding of Exeter's origins. Previously there had been only isolated

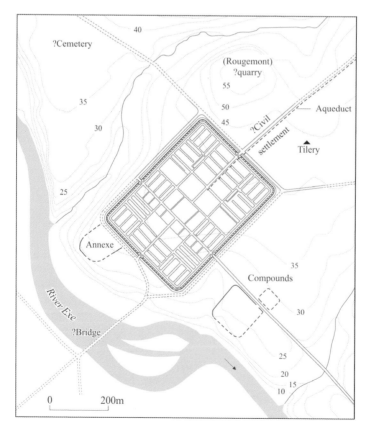

2 The
topographical
setting of the
Roman fortress
c.AD 50-75

3 The excavated legionary bath house by the cathedral's west front in 1973. It was then covered until funds were available to exhibit it.

discoveries relating to the arrival of the Roman army. A tile found in Seaton had shown that the Second Legion (the one commanded by Vespasian) was stationed there in AD 49. Vespasian's biographer records that he fought thirty battles in his campaigns in Britain, conquered two powerful tribes and captured more than twenty native fortresses.

The 1970s brought opportunities for large-scale excavations, not only in the Cathedral Yard but also in the Guildhall area before the shopping precinct was built there. Other excavations took place in Paul Street, Fore Street, Catherine Street and Gandy Street. The Archaeological Field Unit found abundant traces of wooden barrack-blocks packed side by side in the present city centre, the line of the fortress walls and the position of its defensive towers, and, in the Cathedral Yard, substantial remains of a splendid stone-built legionary bath-house, from about AD 55. The bath-house is the oldest cut-and-mortared stone building in Britain. The legion moved on to South Wales after about twenty years, leaving Exeter as a tribal capital like Winchester or Silchester. It was now known as *Isca Dumnoniorum*—'Isca, [capital city] of the Dumnonii'—though the natives no doubt kept their own name for it for many centuries after this. The Romans converted the fortress into a town on the Italian model, with a regular grid-iron street plan, fine public buildings including baths (smaller

4 A clear view of the under-floor heating system of the legionary baths. This *caldarium* (hot room) is the largest yet discovered in Britain. Walls of the later *basilica* cut across it (in the centre of the picture).

5 One of the seven arches carrying hot air from the *caldarium* to the *tepidarium*.

than the legionary bath-house), a basilica or town hall, a forum—the main square and market-place—and other features of a provincial city.

They also did something which determined the layout of Exeter for the next thousand years or more. They built a substantial bank around the town, a rampart of earth about five feet high and over twenty feet wide at the base, with a walk along the top. This bank enclosed a much larger

area than that of the fortress or even
of the Roman town, especially on
the eastern side where it must have
been drawn across waste ground well
outside the built-up area. This bank
was constructed about A.D. 120 or
a little later. And finally, about the
year 200, the bank was superseded
by a wall. The line the Romans drew
for their bank and then their wall
became also the line of the walls
of the medieval city, a line which
largely survives to this day.

6 This fragment of multi-coloured
mosaic from the legionary bath-house
is the earliest piece of mosaic found in
Britain.

The walls erected by the Romans
followed strong natural defences on
two sides. On the north-western side (from what is now Northernhay down
to the Snail Tower near Allhallows churchyard) the wall ran along the top
of a precipitous slope dropping down to the old Long Brook. This brook
was covered in during the 1840s and when the railway reached Exeter in
1860 the valley was also largely filled in. Just below the Central Station, for
example, the made-up ground is over fifty feet in depth. The Long Brook
still flows underground, reaching the mill leat at the end of Exe Street, at
what used to be known as the Horse Pond.

At the Snail Tower the walls turned sharply and ran south-east down
the spur, but kept well above the river on a low cliff which can still be
seen at the Cricklepit Mills.
Beneath this cliff there
stretched a great marsh
or swamp over which the
tide flowed back and forth
in Roman times. Centuries
later this marsh was re-
claimed by constructing
a network of leats which
drained it and also produced
power for several mills.
The drained area became
known as Exe Island. But
under natural conditions in
Roman and Saxon times
it was a formidable barrier
against attack from this
side.

7 Steps leading to the
basilica (civilian town hall);
probably a pillared private
entrance for the magistrates.

cm

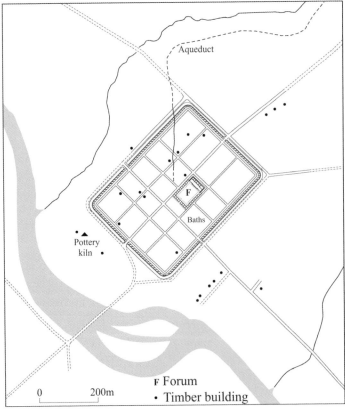

Aqueduct

F

Baths

Pottery
kiln

0   200m

F Forum
• Timber building

8 Decorative tile antefixes from the roof of the legionary bath-house, apparently re-used for the *basilica*.

9 The early Roman town *Isca Dumnoniorum* *c.*AD 75-150. Water was brought in from the St Anne's Well area along the St Sidwell's ridge and circling around Rougemont.

On the other sides of the city the wall did not follow any marked natural feature. Having climbed the steep hill from the Quay (parallel with Quay Lane today) it then ran over fairly level ground (past Southernhay, which did not then exist), turned near the East Gate and then ran up the side of the volcanic hill of Rougemont to complete the circuit. Altogether the wall enclosed an area of just under 93 acres. The total circuit was about 2,600 yards, of which five-sixths are still preserved and mostly easily visible.

Considerable portions of the original Roman masonry can still be seen, especially in West Street and in Southernhay. The Roman work is composed of volcanic stone from Northernhay, quite unlike the rough red sandstone used in medieval

10 Earth bank still standing inside the city walls at 14 Cathedral Close.

11 Later Roman town *c*.AD 150 to early 5th century. Stone gate-houses and the stone city wall were built in the early 3rd century.

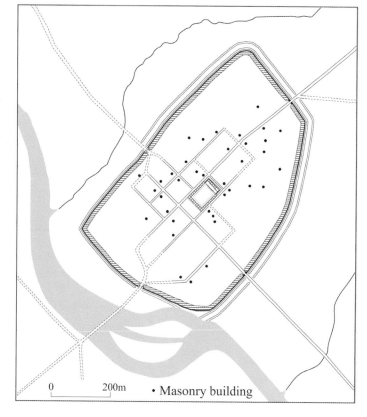

0   200m   • Masonry building

times, and is much more finely jointed than the later work. The bank which preceded the wall can best be seen in Rougemont, backing the city wall, and in the garden of the Bishop's Palace (private).

Roman Roads and Streets

Exeter, though rather smaller than the average tribal capital, was the most important place in the South-West and Roman roads converged upon it. The main route came in from the east. It came up the main street of Heavitree, or very nearly on this line, sighted upon the brow of the hill at Livery Dole.

Here it forked, just as the road does today, one line running down Heavitree Road and up what was Paris Street, to the east gate of the Roman town, and the other running down Magdalen Road. The latter was the main approach to Exeter for many centuries, indeed for well over fifteen hundred years. When kings visited Exeter they always came this way to the South Gate, which was the most important entrance to the city and was often known simply as the Great Gate.

This road—Magdalen Road and Magdalen Street—still runs almost dead straight like a true Roman road. But originally, before the Magdalen Road bridge was made about 1832, it plunged down into a deep valley, almost a ravine, and up the other side before it reached the level ground outside the South Gate.

The *Valiant Soldier* inn, on the corner of Holloway Street and Magdalen Street, stood at what was an important road junction in Roman times. Here three Roman roads met. One came up from Topsham, which was the outport of the city at that time. Another was the main road just described, coming down from the Midlands and Bath. And the third was Quay Lane, which was the direct way from the quay up to the city at the South Gate. The old way from the quay, along the coombe (Coombe Street) into the town, was cut off by the building of the walls. Not for many centuries were the walls pierced to make an additional gate—the Water Gate—so as to re-open the ancient way in.

Roman roads also ran westwards and northwards out of the city. The western road left by the West Gate and went over Haldon to Teignbridge. The northern road left by the North Gate and so over St David's Hill towards North Tawton, probably crossing the Exe at or near the present Cowley Bridge. Another minor road left by the East Gate, went up St Sidwell's and over Stoke Hill, where traces of it may still be seen on the slopes dropping down to Stoke Canon bridge. As there was a Roman signal station on the top of Pennsylvania (just behind what was the Panorama Café), Longbrook Street must also have been a Roman road, of a purely local importance.

Within the city itself we know very little of the Roman street-plan. Short stretches of street have turned up here and there, but most of the grid-iron plan was destroyed long ago by the excavating of cellars in the rich medieval city. High Street was a Roman street, just as it had been the principal track in earlier centuries.

12 The South Gate of Exeter: the principal entrance to the city from Roman times onwards. Demolished in 1819.

The main street out to the west was Smythen Street, with its continuation in Stepcote Hill. It is possible also that Waterbeer Street is Roman in origin, as it runs parallel with High Street. In the summer of 1959, too, some excavations in Bartholomew Street East revealed another short piece of Roman street, running roughly parallel with the present street towards Mary Arches Street about twenty-five yards back on the south side. In time we shall probably be able to piece together these fragments of the street plan of the second century and to draw the complete Roman layout.

Roman Exeter had three cemeteries, outside the north, east, and south gates. That outside the north gate lay just to the north of St David's church and may be the earliest, as many coins of the first century have been found here. The fact that it lay near St David's Hill is evidence for the latter being a Roman road. All the cemeteries were naturally located near a road, for ease of access. The eastern cemetery lay in the neighbourhood of Well Street and York Road, in St Sidwell's, and the southern one in Magdalen Street or very near it, in the neighbourhood of the Acorn roundabout today. The Romano-British buried their dead well outside the inhabited area, unlike the Christian inhabitants of the city who buried all their dead (except a few rich enough to be buried in a church) in the Cathedral Yard. For at least a thousand years this was the only burial-place for the whole city, until the Bartholomew Yard was opened in the year 1637.

CHAPTER TWO

Exeter under the Saxons

The Dark Centuries

THE ROMANS WITHDREW FROM BRITAIN to defend their homeland early in the fifth century. What happened in the British towns after that still remains largely a mystery. In most towns there can be no doubt that all civilised life broke down. The handsome public buildings fell into ruin, streets were left unrepaired, and as time passed became blocked with fallen masonry just like a modern town after an air-raid. Many towns were completely deserted by their inhabitants, especially those on the eastern side of Britain which was wide open to the Anglo-Saxon barbarians from across the North Sea.

In the far west of Britain, however, life probably went on without a break—though not as before. Exeter was never completely deserted, although the built-up area almost certainly shrank in size, and life became more squalid and poverty-stricken. Exeter was too far west to be troubled by the barbarians from ancient Germany (just as it was in 1914-18, but not in 1939-45), and the walled town offered some security in any event.

But it is clear that civilised life must have broken down even in the quiet West, or so we think because there is a complete disappearance of coins before the end of the fourth century. Coins imply trade and a settled and stable government. At Exeter there are practically no coins after about A.D. 380. About 1,100 Roman coins have been found in the city. Probably hundreds more have been found and never recorded, but those of which we have a record furnish a good sample. They show Exeter at its most prosperous in the first half of the fourth century—no fewer than 300 coins belong to this period—but then follows a striking fall. After about 380 only two coins have been recorded.

There is a total silence in the history of Exeter for almost three hundred years: not a single reference in any document anywhere, not a coin or a piece of pottery, not a fragment of a building.

And yet the city must have lived on all through these dark generations. There may be two reasons why we have found nothing to fill this great gap. One is that the inhabited area was so shrunken that we have not yet come across it in excavations, and the other is, that the material culture—the houses, their utensils, their coinage or lack of it—was so miserably poor that it has all perished long ago. Coins and pottery and

14

stone buildings survive long enough to be recognised, but the British who lived on amid the ruins of Roman Exeter were squalid slum-dwellers, possessing nothing that would last their own lifetime, let alone many centuries after them. It is possible, too, that their remains have in fact been unearthed from time to time, but, being so poor, have not been recognised for what they were.

At any rate, the next definite record of the existence of Exeter as a town does not occur until about 680. Then we are told, in a life of St Boniface, who was born near Crediton, that he received his first education in the abbey at Exeter. When had the Saxons reached Exeter, and when was the abbey founded?

The Anglo-Saxons took a long time to conquer the far west of Britain. They did not occupy Exeter until the year 658. They came to terms with the British inhabitants of the city and allowed them to continue living peacefully in their own quarter and under their own laws, while the Saxons occupied another part of the city and had their own laws. There is an exact modern parallel to this division of a city between two different peoples. The city of Montreal in Canada is still divided precisely between the English-speaking and the French-speaking inhabitants. In point of fact there was so much derelict land

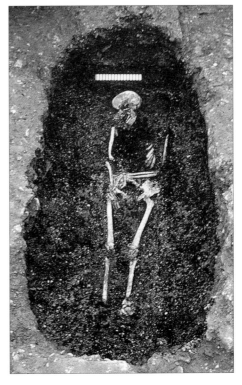

13 Statue of the young Boniface in Newcombes Meadow, Crediton.

14 A Saxon burial in the Cathedral Close. The coffin had been laid on a bed of charcoal, a common practice in Middle and Late Saxon England. The grave had been cut into the floor of the Roman *basilica*.

within the walls of Exeter, and so many ruins to be cleared up, that there was ample room for both peoples. This arrangement continued right down to the tenth century, when Athelstan expelled the British and made Exeter an entirely English city, in all probability about the year 928 when we know he was in the city.

There can be little doubt that the British quarter between 658 and 928 lay in the original area of ancient British settlement, in the district roughly marked by Bartholomew Street today. For centuries during the Middle Ages this street was known as Britayne, a reference to the memory that it was once the British Quarter. In the Saxon Quarter the most splendid building was the abbey dedicated to St Mary and St Peter, which the Saxon king Cenwealh founded in the year 670, on the site of the present cathedral or, more precisely, to the west of it.

The Saxon City and its Setting

In the British Quarter there were poky little winding streets, hardly more than lanes, but in the English or Saxon Quarter the streets were better planned and generally ran straight. In some places the Saxons followed the old Roman streets, but where these were buried under rubble they made new streets just as we did when Exeter was rebuilt after the war of 1939-45.

For nearly three hundred years, then, there were two Exeters within the walls, who probably kept themselves to themselves as the saying is. The British were on the whole the poorer class, earning their living by supplying domestic labour to the richer Saxon households, by fishing in the river, and perhaps by spinning, weaving, and tanning on a small scale.

Not all the British were as lowly as this, however, for we occasionally find a Celtic name among the moneyers (that is, those who were licensed to make money at the Exeter mint) in Saxon times. Coins were first minted at Exeter in the time of King Alfred (871-901) and continued to be minted here until the time of Edward I. We do not know where this early mint was situated. The present street-name The Mint refers to a mint set up in the year 1696 for a short period.

Older citizens of Exeter today will remember what used to be called the West Quarter, a whole area of slums and poverty now happily almost gone. The British Quarter of Exeter a thousand or more years ago must have been rather like that, although the houses then would have been even worse, mere thatched huts strung out along unmade lanes.

15 A silver penny of 'long cross' type issued by the moneyer Wulfsige of Exeter between 997 and 1003, showing the head of King Ethelred the Unready.

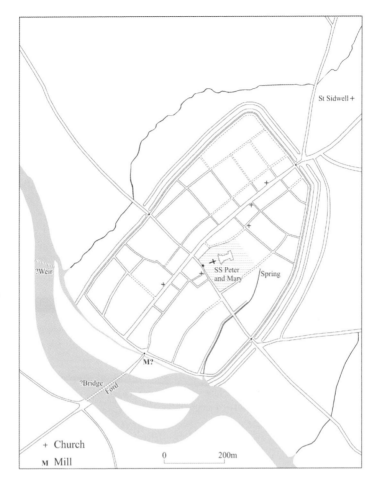

16 Late Saxon
Exeter *c.*880-1068.
The town was
refounded on the
orders of King
Alfred, which
established much
of the street grid
of today's city
centre.

When Devon was conquered by the Saxons in the seventh century, the
Saxon kings took for themselves the richest lands—chiefly the 'red lands'
around Exeter which still fetch the highest prices. They also took over the
walled city of Exeter, which became a royal possession and remained so for
many centuries. But what was the country like outside the walls?

All around the city, enclosing it completely on three sides, with the
river on the fourth, stretched a vast royal estate. We must forget everything
beyond the river to the west, the populous St Thomas district today. This
had no connection with the city for many centuries to come.

The great royal estate that enclosed Exeter like a large fleshy peach
round a tiny stone, was called Wonford. The old village of Wonford today is
almost lost in the modern housing estates all round it, but it is an ancient
name. It is quite possible that this ancient estate of Wonford which passed
into the Saxon king's hands in the year 658 was even older. It may have
been, long before that, a part of the royal estate of the Celtic kings of
Dumnonia, for Exeter, as we have seen, was the tribal capital and Celtic
kings must have held their court here from time to time.

Two miles or so north of the city a massive hedgebank runs from the river (or a branch of it) right up through Stoke Woods, where it can be clearly traced. It crosses the Marypole Head-Stoke Canon road just beyond the summit and continues as a hedgebank until it reaches Stoke Hill Camp, which we know was an Iron-Age fortress, certainly occupied in the first century A.D. if not somewhat earlier. From here the boundary-bank, for such it is, runs along a ridgeway until it meets the old road over Stoke Hill from Exeter. On the other side of this road, near the second milestone from Exeter, is a particularly massive stretch of bank serving no purpose today.

I suspect that this great bank, running all the way from the Exe, marked the boundary of the royal estate of the Dumnonian kings around Exeter. I have not traced it beyond this point, but it probably ran across to Beacon Hill above Pinhoe, a very ancient look-out place. These ancient features do not wholly disappear in the countryside: they remain for those who have eyes to see and who know where to look.

Gradually this great estate around Exeter was reduced in size. Various Saxon kings gave considerable pieces of it to the new abbey, but most of it remained royal land right down to 1066 when William the Conqueror took over from the Saxon kings.

There is, however, one mysterious piece of land near Exeter, and that is Duryard. This belonged to the city from time immemorial right down to the early 18th century when the city fathers, hard up for money as usual, sold it off. The manor of Duryard stretched from the very walls of Exeter northwards to the river opposite Pynes.

Now, Duryard is often thought to mean 'deer park'.* In Domesday Book (compiled in 1086) it already belonged to the city of Exeter. How had the city acquired it?

If it does mean deer-park, the name gives us a clue. Duryard in its natural state consisted of rolling hills, separated by steep-sided wooded coombes like the Longbrook valley, the Hoopern valley, and the Duryard valley itself, a rough country swarming with wild animals. When the Saxon kings visited Exeter, they hunted over this 'door-yard' or rough country outside the walls. It was their 'deer-park', and was probably always regarded as part of the royal city. So when the Normans took over England in 1066 they found a city possessing a large estate outside its walls.

By this time Exeter was paying a tribute, or a sort of rent, to the kings of England of £18 a year. This revenue was usually given by the king to his queen as a wedding gift—it was called a 'morning gift'.

It sounds rather a trivial sum for a whole city to pay for certain privileges but in fact it would be equivalent to perhaps £100,000 or £125,000 a year today [2004]. The payment to the king represented an average levy of about £250 on every inhabited house in terms of money today. Before the 1939-45 war every inhabited house in Exeter paid on an average about £17 to the city council by way of rates, and got a great deal back in the form of various services. So the Saxon city was really paying out a large annual

---

* Or possibly 'door-yard', land outside the gate.

sum with little to show for it except—what was well worth having—a considerable degree of independence.

There were deep wooded valleys right outside the city walls. The Longbrook, with its precipitous slopes dropping down from Rougemont, was wooded for many centuries, while the corresponding valley to the south—which was really an open sewer for the city—was also wooded. The name Larkbeare, which applied to the lower end of this valley, means 'larks' wood', and must be a reference to the number of larks that sang here on summer mornings a thousand years ago where now is only the screech of car brakes and the stink of exhaust fumes.

On the level ground that is now St Sidwell's the citizens, or those who earned their living by farming, cultivated their strips in the open hedgeless fields, while in Duryard—now rarely used for hunting—there were probably small cattle farms from which the city drew a modest revenue.

The Earliest Churches

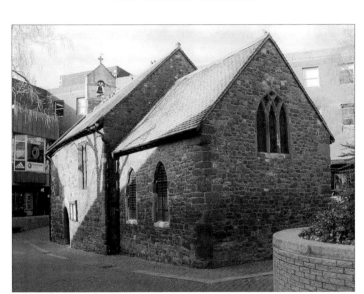

17 St Pancras

Exeter is known today for its little red sandstone churches, scattered about the city within the old walled area. They are not notable as architecture, like some of the parish churches of Norwich, for example; but they are a very pleasant part of the street scene in the modern city. Indeed, it is curious that a city that was once so rich and important never built a single parish church, as far as we know, comparable in size and dignity with, say, St Peter Mancroft at Norwich. We do not know the reason for this lack of fine churches in Exeter.

But what the Exeter churches lacked in splendour they made up in number, for there used to be rather more than thirty churches in the city, of which all but four lay inside the walled area. Those that lay outside were St Sidwell's, St David's, St Leonard's and St Edmund's. Many of these ancient churches vanished long ago, and some have been lost in the last hundred years, such as Allhallows, Goldsmith Street, pulled down in 1906 and St Lawrence's, destroyed by the Germans in 1942.

How did these ancient churches originate and is it possible to say which is the mother of them all?

Christianity reached Britain as long ago as about A.D. 200, and there is evidence that there were Christians in Exeter before the end of the fourth century. The evidence is very scanty, and the Christians were doubtless a small minority in a generally heathen population still worshipping pagan gods. We do not know where in Exeter the earliest Christian church stood, but it is likely that it stood opposite the west front of the present cathedral, on the site of the successive churches called St Mary Major.

There were three churches in Exeter dedicated to St Mary, the Mother of God, and of these three St Mary Major was always so called because it was the senior of them all. Moreover, it stood in the centre of the old city, very near the centre of Roman Exeter, and probably began as the Saxon abbey of St Mary and St Peter.

St Mary Major was demolished in 1971. There was little to be said for it as a building. It dated only from 1865-7, and it had long spoilt the view of the west front of the cathedral. Beneath it the archaeologists found not only the amazing remains of the Roman legionary fortress and the early Roman town, but also evidence of early Christian practice and the abbey which would become Exeter's first cathedral.

They found that little remained of the second, medieval St Mary Major, as the foundations and burial vaults of the third, Victorian, church had cut through its walls. Fortunately we have drawings of the important medieval church building.

The archaeologists found traces beneath it of the first, Anglo-Saxon, church, longer and broader than its successor, with an eastern apse. The chancel had been shortened in the early 12th century, perhaps in 1133 when cathedral status was transferred to the new Norman edifice.

Christian burials were found in the area of the Roman forum, dating to within a century of the Roman withdrawal, and many more from the seventh to the 10th centuries, and again from the 10th to the 12th centuries. The graves clustered round the Mary Major church, indicating that it was Exeter's main Christian centre for many years.

In the 1930s Sir Cyril Fox excavated close to the south wall of the cathedral, behind the Bishop's Palace, and uncovered an ancient pool, formed by damming up a copious spring which rose right beneath the cathedral wall. This spring, which originally flowed down the valley that is now Coombe Street, was known to the Romans, who probably constructed the first dam on the site to give a good supply of drinking water.

The Saxons took over this fine spring and pool. They almost certainly chose their abbey site for this reason, and founded their monastery here. There is good reason for saying that the abbey was founded by King Cenwealh of Wessex in the year 670, so that the cathedral, which is the successor of the abbey on the same site, can claim to be over 1,330 years old.

18 The Norman church of St Mary Major; a 19th-century drawing by Edward Ashworth.

Which are our oldest parish churches? There are half a dozen churches of whose great antiquity we may be quite certain. St Olave's is mentioned in Domesday Book and was probably founded by Gytha, the mother of King Harold, who may have lived in Exeter after the death of her husband, Earl Godwin of Wessex, in 1053.

The earl had a mansion house, as we should call it, in Exeter, which stood somewhere near Allhallows churchyard, and the countess occupied it in her widowhood. It was she who caused the first church of St Olave to be built about the year 1060 or perhaps a few years earlier.

Many private persons like Gytha built churches for themselves and their tenants. St George's, which formerly stood near the top of South Street, was first built in the tenth century, and St Stephen's came soon afterwards. There is Saxon work in the sealed-up crypt beneath the church. Another Saxon church was St Sidwell's, built on the site of the martyrdom of our local saint, Sidwell or Sativola (to give her her Latin name).

St Lawrence's church, which stood in the High Street until 1942, is also believed to have originated in Saxon times, while St Martin's is definitely recorded as having been consecrated on 6 July 1065.

Another vanished church, St Kerrian's, stood in North Street until 1878. Its dedication to an early Celtic saint, a missionary monk of Glastonbury who lived in the sixth century, suggests that here was another of the very ancient churches of Exeter.

Although it lies well outside the old city, the church of St Michael at Heavitree must be mentioned. Though largely a Victorian building today, it is the oldest Christian site outside Exeter, probably first built before the year 700. It is the mother of the churches of Topsham, and of St Leonard's,

19 Heavitree Yew. The present yew tree by the tower of the parish church has been estimated to be a 450-year-old shoot which sprouted from a much older tree which was probably cut down when the tower was first rebuilt in 1541.

St Sidwell's, and St David's in the suburbs of Exeter. It may indeed be a royal foundation, like the abbey within the city, for it stood in the manor of Wonford, which belonged to the Saxon kings for many centuries. One of these kings almost certainly caused a church to be built on his estate near a tree which had some sacred associations. Hence the name Heavitree, Anglo-Saxon *heafod treow*, 'head tree', marking the ruler's 'capital' meeting place.

The Danes

England was much troubled by the Danes for about two hundred years. These uncouth characters need not detain us long, for they made no lasting impression on the city of Exeter, less probably than the Germans after 1942. They captured Exeter in the autumn of 876 and spent the winter and following spring here, being thrown out by Alfred in the summer. The fact that they had broken in so easily suggests that the Roman walls were in a state of disrepair, possibly even fallen in places. Centuries of neglected ivy would have been sufficient to do this. At any rate, Athelstan repaired the walls throughout some fifty years later (about the year 928), so much so that he has ever since been wrongly regarded as the original builder. At the same time he expelled the British from the city, probably settling them over the Tamar in Cornwall. The empty quarter in which they had lived, or part of it, seems to have been adapted as 'the earl's burh'. It was still called Irlesberi in the 12th century though by then the locality was almost forgotten. It was here that Gytha, the widow of Godwin, lived in the middle years of the 11th century.

The Danes returned to Exeter over a hundred years later, in the year 1001. Now the walls were strong enough to hold out against them, and they were obliged to turn their attention to the defenceless countryside. But two years later they came back to avenge a massacre of the Danes in England, and for some reason attacked Exeter first. This time the city was betrayed into their hands. It belonged to Emma, the queen of Ethelred II, as part of her dowry, with a Frenchman (one Hugh) acting as her reeve or rent-collector. It was he who, again for some unknown reason, opened a gate and let the barbarians in. They burnt and plundered much of the city, including the abbey, and then departed. Slowly the ruined city was rebuilt and resumed its old life. Foreign merchants came back to it (mostly from just across the Channel) and country-people returned to its markets, as they had done from time immemorial and as they still do. The same little local industries picked up again—tanning, weaving, building, and farming—on the outskirts. The Danes became a dim memory with which old men bored the younger generation, and then were eventually forgotten altogether.

CHAPTER THREE

The Normans and after

The Siege of Exeter, 1068

WHEN THE NORMANS took over England in 1066 they found at Exeter a settlement already some 1,200 years old. Its Roman walls had been repaired and were now powerful enough to hold out against the strongest enemy, as William the Conqueror himself was to find a couple of years later.

For the first time in its history, we really know how big Exeter was. It had in 1066 about 460 houses, with a total population of about 2,500. That is, it was about as big as Ashburton or Chudleigh are today. This makes it sound trivial, but in fact it was the tenth biggest town in England at this time and one of the leading cities of the country. It was even more important than its numbers would suggest, for we are told it paid no geld except when London, York, and Winchester paid. It was, in fact, still the capital city of the West, as it had been ever since Roman times.

The abbey had disappeared. It had been destroyed by the Danes under King Sweyn when he had ravaged and set fire to the city in the year 1003. This was the biggest disaster until the burning of the city by the Germans in 1942.

The abbey had been rebuilt, just as we have rebuilt much of our burnt city; but in the year 1050 it became a cathedral when Bishop Leofric was allowed by the Pope to transfer his see from Crediton to Exeter. The eight Benedictine monks who were here at the time were transferred to Westminster Abbey, and the secular canons took over the monastic buildings and church.

Probably the street-plan of Exeter as we knew it in 1939 had already been laid out. Certainly all our major streets were there when the Normans came, and so were most of the lesser streets and lanes. Though so small in numbers, Exeter was a rich trading city, visited by foreign merchants and with wealthy merchants of its own.

Somewhere in the city a gild hall already existed, for we know there was a gild in Exeter by the year 1000. It is sometimes said that the first gild hall stood in Waterbeer Street, but I do not know of any evidence for saying this, and it is more likely that it stood where the present Guildhall stands today.

Thus there was a small Saxon cathedral, standing to the west of the present cathedral, and a Saxon gildhall in the High Street, when the

24

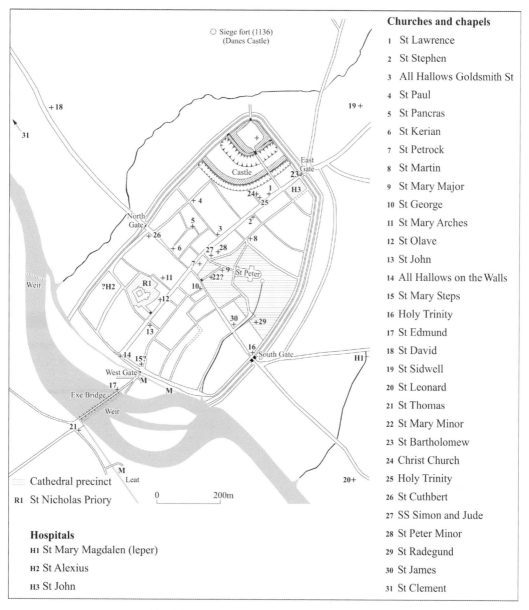

○ Siege fort (1136)
(Danes Castle)

Churches and chapels

1   St Lawrence
2   St Stephen
3   All Hallows Goldsmith St
4   St Paul
5   St Pancras
6   St Kerian
7   St Petrock
8   St Martin
9   St Mary Major
10 St George
11 St Mary Arches
12 St Olave
13 St John
14 All Hallows on the Walls
15 St Mary Steps
16 Holy Trinity
17 St Edmund
18 St David
19 St Sidwell
20 St Leonard
21 St Thomas
22 St Mary Minor
23 St Bartholomew
24 Christ Church
25 Holy Trinity
26 St Cuthbert
27 SS Simon and Jude
28 St Peter Minor
29 St Radegund
30 St James
31 St Clement

Cathedral precinct
R1 St Nicholas Priory

Hospitals
H1 St Mary Magdalen (leper)
H2 St Alexius
H3 St John

20   Norman Exeter *c.*1068-1220

Normans took over. But the third great feature of early Exeter—Exeter Castle—did not exist in 1066.

The volcanic hill on which the castle was to be built, later to be called Rougemont, had little houses built on it, though perhaps there was an open space at the top. It was the Normans who first saw the military possibilities of this hill, rising as it does some sixty or seventy feet above the plateau on which the city mainly stood. But they did not perceive these possibilities until Exeter had carried out a successful rebellion against the Conqueror less than eighteen months after the battle of Hastings.

I have told the story of this defiance of William in *Devon and its People*, but it is necessary to say something about it again as it is an important part of the history of Exeter.

Gytha, the mother of Harold, the last of our Saxon kings, was either living in Exeter at the time of the battle of Hastings, or fled here immediately afterwards. At any rate, she was here shortly after the battle, and perhaps became the centre of a dangerous resistance movement to William. Or perhaps the real cause of Exeter's resistance was simply William's demand that the ancient tribute of £18 a year should be increased.

He returned in haste from Normandy and demanded that the city should swear an oath of fealty to him. The citizens replied that they would neither swear allegiance to him nor admit him within their walls. They would pay him tribute according to ancient custom, but not a penny more.

The enraged William marched westwards in person. The governing body of the city grew alarmed, went to meet him about four miles out where he had halted, and gave him hostages for the good behaviour of the city. But when they returned to their fellow citizens, their bargain was repudiated, and the walls and gates were put in readiness for a siege. William appeared before the South Gate and caused one of the hostages to be blinded before the citizens who lined the walls. The only answer was an obscene gesture from one of the more uncouth defenders, which vastly increased the king's rage. For 18 days he surrounded the city, tried to undermine its walls, and attacked day after day without success.

The citizens were suffering greatly from the siege, but so was William. Until Exeter was dealt with, there was the risk of a rebellion throughout the South-West, and he could not afford to wait in midwinter for the city to capitulate.

The result was an honourable surrender, in which William was obliged to swear a solemn oath on the sacred books of the cathedral that he would not harm the city in any way, nor would he increase its ancient tribute. And with this he hurried away into Cornwall to quell trouble down there.

But there were to be no more risks. The Norman military engineers turned up and selected a site for a castle. Work was begun immediately, and 48 houses on the hill were demolished to get the necessary space for the outworks.

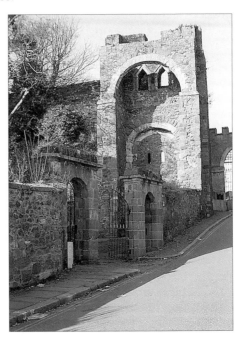

21 The gate-house of Rougemont Castle.

The gatehouse of this Norman castle still stands at the top of Castle Street, built in the year 1068, and one of the finest pieces of Norman military architecture in England.

In the meantime, Gytha and her daughter were allowed to leave Exeter without harm, and never came back again. The properties of the Saxon landlords in the city passed into the hands of Norman landlords, bishops, and soldiers, and when Bishop Leofric died in 1072 a Norman—Osbern Fitz-Osbern—was appointed in his place.

King William was the biggest landlord in Exeter, owning 285 houses or nearly three-quarters of the entire city. The Norman grip was a tight one, but there was a certain amount of compromise with a proud and ancient city, for it looks as though the chief citizens—the portreeves—continued to be Saxons for a good while afterwards. We do not know many of their names, but such as we know are pure Saxon, like Aelfger and Alword and Saerla.

Cathedral and Parish Churches

The century following the Norman Conquest was a period of rapid growth and change for the city of Exeter. According to one chronicler, it was the fourth city in England in wealth and reputation, only surpassed by London, York, and Winchester.

William of Malmesbury, writing about 1125, says that the city was planted on a barren soil, which hardly produced even oats (one can only wonder which way he came to Exeter and how long he stayed to have this mistaken impression). But, he goes on, the greatness of the city, the concourse of strangers, the wealth of the citizens, and the abundance of good things from all parts of the world, leave nothing to be desired. Exeter was thronged with foreign merchants, for the tide still came up to the walls, the river was unimpeded by weirs, and ships could reach the quay as they had done since pre-historic times.

A great new Norman cathedral was rising on the top of the hill from the year 1112 onwards, its fresh-cut Beer stone shining in the sun in a way we can hardly imagine today. The Saxon minster was of course still standing when the Norman cathedral was begun, and it was left in use until the cathedral was sufficiently finished to be ready in its turn. It stood, as we have seen, to the west of the new cathedral. In June 1133, the canons left the old building and entered into the new.

Most of this Norman building, which was completed in the time of Bishop Marshall (1194-1206) is now obscured by the later and grander rebuilding of the 13th and 14th centuries—all except the magnificent Norman towers, transeptal towers unique among English cathedrals which give us the superb internal line of roof unbroken by any central tower.

We have a good idea of the size of the Norman cathedral. It was of the same width as the present building, but not as long. It ran from the present west front to a point three bays east of the present crossing, almost exactly two-thirds of the length of the cathedral as it is today.

Not only did the city receive a shining new cathedral, but many more parish churches were being built, by private benefactors for the most part.

22 The font in the church of St Mary Steps.

Several of the Exeter churches were in existence before the Norman Conquest, but many more were first erected during the 12th century.

It looks, for example, as if St Mary Steps, at the foot of Stepcote Hill, was first built about 1150. Like nearly all the Exeter churches, it was rebuilt in the 15th century, but it retains its Norman font as ancient evidence of its right to baptise, and this gives us a date for the first church. There may have been a little church here before 1150, but this is unlikely as this part of the city was not fully developed until about that time.

So many churches and chapels were built during the 12th century that by the end there were no fewer than 32 in existence. One of the new churches of this period was St Leonard, well outside the South Gate. This was in existence by 1140, possibly a little earlier.

The Growth of Exe Island

Another important development during the 12th century was the reclamation of the marsh between the foot of the hill and the river, the part that we call Exe Island today. The river was much wider then than now, flowing as far east as Frog Street, and was flanked by mud flats over which high tides flowed. This swamp was valuable as a natural defence in early times, but as the city grew it was simply a waste and a hindrance to growth. So we get the cutting of the first leat or water course, still a feature of this part of the city, in order to drain this bad land and make it usable.

The oldest of these leats, beyond much doubt, is that which comes off the river near Head Weir and flows below the city walls to rejoin the river at the Quay. This leat was nearly half a mile long. It certainly existed by the middle of the 12th century, and was quite possibly first made in the 10th century. We know that the Saxons were capable of large-scale drainage operations in the Fens and elsewhere, and there is no reason to doubt their capabilities at Exeter. This leat, now a thousand years old, created Exe Island, and Exe Island became a separate manor belonging to the earls of Devon, whose property thus extended to the foot of the city walls.

As time went on, more leats were cut through this low-lying land, and the course of the river was narrowed down. All these leats are of great age, and form a very interesting and picturesque part of Exeter, too infrequently visited. Not only did the leats drain the swampy land between the city walls and the river, but they provided a valuable source of water-power for the cloth mills of the city.

Exeter was one of the leading cloth-towns of England by the end of the 12th century. In the year 1202 we find recorded the payments from various towns to the king so that their merchants might buy and sell coloured cloth as they used to do in the time of King Henry II (1154-89). Lincoln, York, and Beverley paid the highest sums, then Leicester, Northampton, and Winchester, and Exeter came into a third group with Stamford, Newcastle, and Gloucester.

About the same time we hear of a flourishing wine trade at Exeter. In the pipe roll for 1199 'the vintners of Exeter' are put down as owing 20 marks (£13 6s. 8d.*) for their fine. We do not know what their offence had been, but it was certainly a substantial fine. The wine trade was already an old one at Exeter,

23 Tillet block used to stamp bales of woollen goods packed for export.

the earliest link being with Rouen, just across the Channel, which had a monopoly of the export of French wines from the interior. Pottery has been found in Exeter which almost certainly came across from Rouen in the 11th or 12th centuries.

When William Sukespic, a successful Exeter merchant who flourished from about 1150 to 1190, bought a small estate from Henry de la Pomeroy at Clyst St George, the transaction was sealed, so to speak, with the gift from William to Henry of a cask of wine. The acquisition of Gascony by the English crown, by the marriage of Henry II to Eleanor of Aquitaine, also increased the wine trade at Exeter—this time claret from Bordeaux. It is gratifying to think that claret has been drunk in Exeter for the past eight hundred years, though it is now many years, alas, since the last cargo of wine came by ship up to Exeter Quay. The city levied its own customs duty of fourpence on every cask of red wine imported and so raised a considerable revenue.

To return from wine to water, however, the medieval leats were lined with fulling mills, corn mills, and tanneries, and perhaps breweries also. The earliest reference to mills in this industrial part of Exeter occurs in a document in the city's Record Office. It is undated, but the names of the witnesses tell us that it was written between 1180 and 1190.

* Decimal currency did not come in until 1971. Until then, people used pounds, shillings and pence, £.s.d. There were twelve pence to a shilling, and twenty shillings to a pound.

24 Puzzle jug made in south-west France *c*.1300 and found in South Street.

It is a grant by Robert de Courtenay, who owned this land, to Nicholas Gervase of 'all his water which Thomas the Fuller holds of him outside the west gate of Exeter, which is between his corn mills and Crickenpette, so that the said Nicholas and his heirs may build a mill on the said water towards Crikenpette as shall appear best and most commodious to them'.

Until most of the leats were piped and covered in the 1960s the City Mills of Messrs French stood where the Courtenays had their mills. The new mill built by Nicholas Gervase in 1180-90 is still represented by Cricklepit Mills.

By the end of the 12th century Exe Island had become the chief industrial quarter of Exeter, and the Courtenays had a rich piece of property.

Up in the city proper, new streets were being built and rapidly filled up with craftsmen, merchants, artisans, and shop-keepers, many groups having their own particular street, like the smiths in Smythen Street, the milk sellers in Milk Street, and the goldsmiths in Goldsmith Street.

Exeter Castle

The Normans were the first to build on the volcanic hill that we call Rougemont today. The Saxons and earlier people had their fortified position at the end of the spur, roughly where the disused churchyard of Allhallows-on-the-Walls lies today. This was not only the site of the pre-historic earthwork, but was also the area occupied by the 'Earl's Burh' in late Saxon times. Almost certainly the great Earl Godwin of Wessex had his fortified house somewhere round here.

It is curious that no one seems to have fortified the hill of Rougemont before the Normans, but the fact is that the Saxon burh, though not so high as Rougemont, commanded a better view of the river.

William the Conqueror gave orders for the building of a castle in Exeter in the year 1068. Work was begun immediately, and a great gate-house built, cut off from the city by a high bank and a deep ditch, which we can still see (though partly filled) in Rougemont Gardens today. This ditch cut off the castle area from the rest of the city, and was crossed by a drawbridge. Outside this inner ward, a second or outer ward was constructed. This, too, was cut off from the city by a bank and ditch, which is more difficult to trace today because it has been partly levelled in order to take later buildings. But the steep slope at the entrance to the Phoenix Arts Centre in Gandy Street marks the line of this bank at that point.

The making of the castle must have occupied a considerable period. It was finished sufficiently to withstand a great siege in the year 1136, but we still read of much money being spent on further work in 1170-1 and again in 1204-8.

In the latter year, stone and lime were brought in great quantities 'for making the ditch of the castle'. This ditch must have been made quite early on as an essential part of the defences, and in 1208 it was being faced with stone in order to strengthen it.

Exeter Castle belonged to the king from the beginning, though he committed it to the care of the Sheriff of Devon. It is always called Exeter Castle in the national records, but locally it began to be called Rougemont. This name first appears in a record among the Dean and Chapter archives about the year 1250, and it has been known by that name in Exeter ever since. It means, of course, 'the red hill', from the colour of the rock here.

In the year 1136 Exeter Castle was the scene of one of the most dramatic episodes in the history of the city. When Henry I died, he left behind a daughter, Matilda, and a nephew, Stephen, who disputed for the succession to the throne. England was plunged into civil war in which the great barons took sides. The Earl of Devon (Baldwin de Redvers) supported Matilda, though it is likely also that he had a private grievance against King Stephen. As a first move in the West, Baldwin occupied Exeter Castle with his own army.

It was by now a fortress of great strength, surrounded by a wall of immense thickness and protected by two deep ditches. The citizens of Exeter appealed to the king against this occupation by Baldwin, who had required them to acknowledge his sole authority.

The message reached the King, who set off at once for Exeter. Baldwin's followers plundered and burnt a certain part of the city and then retired to await the arrival of the King's forces. The castle was well garrisoned and fully provisioned. Two wells in the inner courtyard supplied all the water that would be needed for a siege. For three months Stephen's army tried by every device to break into the castle. They met with an early success when they captured an outwork which had been raised, we are told, on a very big mound to defend the castle.

This outwork has always puzzled historians of Exeter, but there seems to be no doubt that it was what we call Danes Castle today. The reservoir behind the prison was moved in 1992, revealing a small military earthwork, clearly of Norman origin. What makes it more certain is that, in the 13th-century deeds among the city records and right down to Elizabethan times, it is called 'the New Castle'. When we find it called 'the New Castle' as far back as about 1260, we can be sure that it was so called in relation to Rougemont, which would have been 'the Old Castle'. The earthwork has nothing at all to do with the Danes. Danes Castle is a name which crept in during the 18th century, when much was attributed to the Danes, who seem to have exercised a strange fascination for 18th-century antiquaries.

Despite Stephen's early success, Baldwin still held out in Exeter Castle. The king brought in miners to tunnel under the outer walls, but without success. When the old Hippodrome was demolished in the 1930s and the ground excavated for the foundations of a new building, a tunnel was found at great depth running from outside the city wall towards the castle. This was thought to be one of the tunnels made by Stephen's mining engineers eight hundred and more years ago.

The weeks dragged by. The King had spent a fortune in trying to capture the castle. Then the castle wells ran dry, though they had never been known to fail before. Probably they had not had to stand so much use with all the men, horses, and cattle inside the castle for three months on end. The chronicler of the siege tells us that the castle still tried to hold out.

The garrison had large supplies of wine. They used this not only for drinking, but also for baking and cooking, and even for extinguishing the fires started by the besiegers throwing in flaming torches.

At last the wine, too, gave out, and Baldwin sent a deputation to Stephen promising to surrender the castle on condition that their lives were spared. Stephen at first refused this condition but, under pressure from his own army, eventually gave way and allowed the besieged garrison to march out.

The vast estates of Baldwin were confiscated, and he departed into exile. He was back in England within three years, when he occupied Corfe Castle, in Dorset. He seems to have made his peace with the King, however, and to have resumed his position as Earl of Devon, as in the year 1141 he founded the little priory of St James just outside the city of Exeter for a prior and four monks.

This little priory disappeared long ago, and no traces of it remain except in a few place-names near the river. It is commemorated also in the name of the Priory School in that part of Exeter.

The Building of Exe Bridge

The first we definitely hear of a bridge over the Exe at Exeter is in the year 1196. But a bridge must have existed long before that, for there was a Roman road going out of the West Gate over Haldon to Teignbridge and beyond, and it is unlikely that no bridge existed then. We know that there was a timber bridge over the Thames in Roman London. Pretty certainly there was a similar bridge over the Exe.

Before the first stone bridge was built, Hooker (the first of the historians of Exeter) tells us that the river was crossed by 'certain clappers of timber' for foot-passengers only. Carts and horsemen crossed the river by a ford at low water. This is no mere guess. There exists a fine and accurate (so far as we can tell) drawing of the old Exe Bridge—the first stone bridge—done by W. Schellinks in 1662 and now in the National Library of Austria in Vienna. This shows horsemen and loaded packhorses fording the river just below the bridge. The river was much shallower then than now, when it has been confined between retaining walls, but its current appears to have been much swifter and in times of flood it must have been impassable or at least very dangerous.

The building of the first stone bridge over the Exe is always attributed to Walter Gervase, who was mayor of the city from 1236 to 1238, and who died in 1257. But the story is a longer and more interesting one than that. In the first place the building of the bridge was well advanced as early as 1196 as there exists a document of that year witnessed by 'the chaplain of the bridge'.

25 The medieval Exe Bridge, drawn by W. Schellinks in the summer of 1662

There can hardly have been a chaplain for a wooden footbridge, nor would there have been a chaplain for a bridge not yet in existence. So we may say that the first stone bridge over the Exe was begun perhaps about 1190, at a time when several other stone bridges were being built in England.

The earliest stone bridge was, as we might expect, that over the Thames at London. This was begun by Peter de Colechurch in 1176, inspired perhaps by the Frères Pontifes, who had built several famous bridges on the Continent, including that at Avignon, which still stands, though much broken. London Bridge was still unfinished in 1201, when King John advised the Lord Mayor to call in an eminent French bridge builder to complete the task, so we may conclude that the building of London Bridge took at least thirty years and possibly a little longer than that. Almost at the same time, stone bridges were being built at York, at Durham, and at Lincoln.

Hooker tells us that Nicholas Gervase and his son Walter were the two men primarily responsible for the completion of the Exe Bridge. They observed the dangers of the old footbridge in winter and the fact that many people perished in the flood waters, and they resolved to build something safer and better. But reckoning up the cost they found it an impossible undertaking for one family, however rich.

Walter, the son, therefore made a general collection throughout the country while his father remained in Exeter and saw to the building operations. According to Hooker, Walter Gervase collected ten thousand marks, especially from cardinals and bishops, sufficient not only to finish the bridge but also to purchase lands for its endowment; that is, to keep it in good repair for ever.

Nicholas Gervase died before the work was completed and was buried, together with his wife, in the chapel of St Edmund on the bridge he had so liberally helped to create. St Edmund's chapel (or church) was in existence by 1214 (and perhaps earlier if the chaplain recorded in 1196 officiated there). Nicholas Gervase fades out of the city records in 1228, so we may assume he died about then. Thus the building of the bridge had already been going on for well over thirty years, and probably took another ten years to complete. Nicholas Gervase was the founder of the bridge. He was flourishing from about 1180 onwards, and he had mills and workshops in this part of Exeter. The Gervases were a well-to-do merchant family. Undoubtedly it is to them that we owe the first stone bridge over the river.

The 20th-century bridge was just over 170 feet long. The old Exe Bridge was a much grander affair. It ran, as most people know, on a different line from that one, in a line with the West Gate, across the river diagonally, finishing up, like the 20th-century bridge, on a line with Cowick Street.

We do not know its exact length as we are not sure where it began on the city side. It probably began just outside the West Gate. All this ground was formerly a waterlogged marsh, beginning to be reclaimed in the 12th century, and Frog Street was probably the river bank then—a muddy strand on which a multitude of frogs disported in the medieval rain. The bridge was therefore at least 700 feet long, so it was four times as long as the bridge we have today. Schellink's drawing shows ten arches from the west (St Thomas) side as far as St Edmund's church. Two more arches are to be seen under the church, almost certainly of 12th-century date for they are semi-circular in shape, and there were other arches to the east of the church (towards the West Gate). The old bridge probably had 18 arches. London Bridge had 19 arches and was 905 feet long and 20 feet wide. Exe Bridge was 16½ feet wide, with a carriageway of about twelve feet.

Soon after the bridge was finished a troublesome situation arose. We are told in a legal record dated 1249 that a certain female hermit had shut herself up 'on the bridge of Exe' and was obstructing the traffic. Carts could not get by, to the grave damage of the city's trade. We do not know what kind of structure this thoughtless female had shut herself in to cause all

26 Edmund Street about 1825 from a pencil drawing by John Gendall. The 'street' consisted of the first Exe bridge.

27   Remnants of St Edmund's church and the surviving half of the medieval Exe bridge in 2004.

28   Old Exebridge and public garden.

this annoyance, but whatever it was the city authorities were very patient. They had complained to the justices five years earlier, and nothing had been done. Nor do we know what happened to their second complaint. Whatever parking troubles face a modern city council, they do not have to deal with infuriating female hermits parked for years on end in the middle of a busy bridge.

The old Exe Bridge is always said to have been demolished in 1778, when the new bridge was opened, having stood for nearly six hundred years. But the demolition only applied to the arches over the river. When the City Brewery and other buildings were cleared away, the street they stood along, Edmund Street, was revealed as the surviving half of the medieval bridge. For the Silver Jubilee in 1977 a public park was laid out here.

CHAPTER FOUR

Exeter in the Middle Ages

The Earliest Mayors

HOW WAS EXETER GOVERNED in the distant past? There was no city council as we know it, no mayor, and no permanent city officials. These gradually emerge during the 13th century. Our main difficulty in answering this question is that the civic records, though probably the finest collection outside the City of London, are not numerous enough before about 1160 to enable us to trace the beginnings of things.

The chief officer was at first called the portreeve, as he is still called in some little towns to this day which have never achieved the dignity of a mayor. We know the names of very few of them. By about 1160 there were two chief officers, known as provosts (*prepositi*), and then, quite suddenly, we discover that Exeter has a mayor, one of the first three cities in England to attain this dignity.

As we would expect, London was the first city to achieve this distinction, in 1191 or 1192. Winchester, once the capital of England, had a mayor by the year 1200, and next came Exeter, which certainly had a mayor in 1205, and possibly a year or two before that.

As a matter of interest, Lincoln came next (1206), and then, rather surprisingly, the town of Barnstaple, with a mayor as early as 1210—earlier than either Oxford or York, or many other notable cities.

The name of the earliest mayor of Exeter is not known for certain, but it was probably Martin Prudom, who had been provost some years before. In the earliest years it is very noticeable how the same man was chosen mayor for several years running. Thus William Derling was chosen no fewer than 11 times between about 1208 and 1222. Then Hilary Blund had a long run from 1224 to 1230, and was mayor again in 1234. Martin Rof was mayor no fewer than 15 times between about 1232 and 1253, Adam de Rifford five times (1246-54); then Philip Tinctor had a long run from 1255 to 1263 with eight successive mayoralties.

Incidentally, Tinctor means 'dyer', and reflects the fact that Exeter was still an important cloth-making town. In the first sixty years the mayoralty was filled by only 14 different men. This preference for the same man year after year is curious, but perhaps understandable at that date. Good men were comparatively scarce in a small population. Even now, in the 13th century, Exeter probably had no more than four or five thousand people.

In the latter part of the century we find one Alured de Porta chosen mayor. He first appears in 1276, and was chosen six times subsequently. He is unique among our mayors in that he was hanged as a felon while still in office, on St Stephen's Day (26 December), 1285. For several weeks after this crisis the city was without a mayor until David Cissor (tailor) was chosen at the beginning of Lent.

The execution of Alured de Porta, mayor of an important city, has always been a bit of a mystery, but he appears to have been implicated in the murder of a high official of the cathedral, the precentor Walter Lechlade. The latter had just left matins at the cathedral, between one and two o'clock in the morning (then the customary hour) of 5 November 1283. In the darkness he was set on by a number of men and brutally killed.

It is a long and complicated story of ecclesiastical intrigue, involving a bitter feud between the bishop and the dean. At any rate, one ecclesiastical party, with the sympathy of some important people in the city, decided to 'remove' Lechlade, the new precentor, in the American fashion. Among those involved in the crime were the vicars of Heavitree and Ottery St Mary, and men in the employment of the mayor. At the subsequent inquest, no fewer than 21 men were named as involved in the murder, but for various legal technicalities no one was brought to book.

Two years later, Bishop Quinel (whose adherent Walter Lechlade had been) appealed directly to the King himself—Edward I—who decided to travel to Exeter in person, with his Queen, in order to settle the bitterness between the bishop and the mayor.

They reached Exeter on 22 December and stayed at the castle in great state. The next day was Sunday, when the King and Queen attended mass at the cathedral. On Monday (24 December) the trial was begun in the great hall of the castle. Among the prisoners were the mayor of the city and the dean. The trial was adjourned on Christmas Day and resumed on the 26th.

It went on for several days. A record made two years later states, however, that the mayor was hanged on the 26th. If so, he must have been found guilty from the first and taken straight out to execution, a swift and fierce justice. The actual murderers had escaped, but five people, including the mayor, were hanged for their complicity in the crime. The dean pleaded benefit of clergy and was handed over to the bishop for punishment. He was banished to a monastery—we do not know which one—and eventually died there.

The King and Queen dined with the bishop on Sunday, 30 December. The very door through which they walked into the palace is still there. At this meeting, in all probability, it was decided that the bishop should be permitted to enclose the cathedral churchyard by a wall 12 feet high, as had been done at Lincoln and York, and in London. There were to be gates through the walls, which would be open from dawn till dusk and then locked for the night. The wall and gates were duly made. The principal gates from the city into the Cathedral Yard were Broadgate, St Martin's Gate, and Palace Gate, and there were a number of smaller ones like St Katherine's Gate (formerly Bickleigh Gate) and Bear Gate. These gates stood until the early 19th century.

The high wall around the close or churchyard was the visible symbol of the two jurisdictions in the city—that of the bishop and that of the city proper—between which there had been continual friction, culminating in the murder of the precentor. So the two authorities were clearly demarcated, just as clearly as the royal castle was separated from the city by its own great stone walls. The building of the close wall did not end the ancient friction between the city and the cathedral, but it eased it for the time being.

The Beginnings of a University

Much happened in a busy city like Exeter during the 13th century, but even at that early date one important institution was already a fading memory. There was very nearly a university at Exeter as early as the reign of Henry II. It failed to materialise, probably because Oxford was coming into existence at the same time and eventually began to attract scholars and students from all over the country.

The evidence for detecting the beginnings of a university at Exeter is very slight, but it is fairly conclusive. It occurs in the cartulary of St John's Hospital, still in the city's records, where we read of a grant by Gilbert le Blond (or Gilbert Blund) to the hospital of a rent of 2s. a year from shops in Smythen Street 'where the schools used to be'. Gilbert Blund was one of the provosts of the city in 1225 and his grant probably dates from about this time.

The expression 'the schools' means something much more than 'a school'. They were a place at which learned teachers gathered, to which they attracted students, and out of such schools the great universities of Oxford and Cambridge finally developed.

There were similar 'schools' in some other English towns, but the rise of Oxford, with its central position in Southern England and its easy access to and from London, frustrated all of them, including Exeter. By the 1220s the incipient university of Exeter had become a memory, and its site was occupied by shops.

Smythen Street, now and for a long time past in the poorest part of the city, may seem an odd place in which to find the beginning of a university, but in medieval times this part of the city was richer and more important. There was probably a good reason why the schools should have been here, and that was that here, too, in a street running parallel with Smythen Street, lived all or most of the priests of the city—Preston Street means 'the street of the priests'.

The clergy of Exeter would have been the most learned men in the city, and indeed some of them must have had a national reputation if they were attracting scholars from elsewhere in England. One of these learned Exonians was probably Joseph Iscanus (Joseph of Exeter) who flourished towards the end of the 12th century and wrote Latin poetry.

It is now quite impossible to say exactly where in Smythen Street 'the schools' were, but they were pretty certainly there because of the proximity of the clergy in the neighbouring street. Perhaps they were somewhere near

King Street, formerly called Idle Lane, which connected Smythen Street and Preston Street, and was indeed the only link between the two in medieval times.

Parish Boundaries

The existence of all the clergy, other than the cathedral clergy, in one street like this is also curious, but there was a good reason for it. Though Exeter had so many churches scattered all over it, these churches had no clearly-defined territory: that is, there were no clearly-defined parishes as we understand the term. And as there were no defined parishes, so there could be no rectory or vicarage houses. Priests, therefore, tended to congregate together in one street like any other specialists.

In the year 1222, however, parish boundaries were drawn and parish churches appointed. The boundaries followed by these ancient parishes are very revealing. Where they follow streets and lanes they tell us that those streets and lanes were in existence as early as 1222, and in most cases long before that.

The ecclesiastical parish boundaries of Exeter were revised in 1956, ancient parishes were amalgamated, and other changes made. But the old boundaries still remain on the map as valuable evidence of the topography of the city some seven hundred or more years ago, and they present some nice puzzles when we look at them in detail.

Even as long ago as 1222, the boundaries were not drawn in a neat and tidy way, especially in the heart of the city. To take only one curiosity, for example: the old parish of St Martin forms a neat island of property bounded by High Street, Broadgate, Cathedral Yard, and St Martin's Lane, all very logical indeed: but why does the boundary suddenly shoot across the High Street and take in two properties on the Guildhall side? These are Nos. 197 (now Stead and Simpson) and 198 (now Ann Summers). These two adjoining properties have been in St Martin's parish for nearly 750 years, and it remains a mystery why they were put there in the first place. There must have been some good reason for this at the time, but what it was we shall probably never know.

Some of the parishes created in 1222 have disappeared long ago. How many people know where the parish of St Cuthbert was, or the ancient parish of St James? The church of St Cuthbert stood just inside the North Gate, in a corresponding position to that of Holy Trinity inside the South Gate, and the parish was joined with that of St Paul in March 1285, because of the poverty of both parishes.

In the same way the small, poor parish of St James was absorbed into that of Holy Trinity, perhaps after the disaster of the Black Death. The church, which stood at or near the corner of South Street and Palace Gate, is mentioned in 1312, but in a document of 1387 there is reference only to 'the waste place where the church of St James formerly stood'.

Many other old Exeter churches have perished, at various dates. A full list will be found in Mrs Rose-Troup's *Lost Chapels of Exeter*, published in 1923, though she is mistaken in including St Mary Minor among those that have disappeared. There can be no doubt that St Mary Minor was the original name for St Mary Steps, so called in relation to St Mary Major, the senior of the Exeter churches dedicated to St Mary.

The Underground Passages

One other important piece of topography in 13th-century Exeter is worth mentioning, and that is the so-called underground passages. These are really the underground water supply of the city and are first heard of in a document dated 1226. They were probably first constructed about 1200 when the internal supplies of water from wells and springs was proving inadequate for the rapidly growing city. There is no evidence for saying that they are Roman in origin.

A copious spring was tapped up in St Sidwell's, actually at Lions Holt, and more precisely still where the Southern Railway emerges from the Mount Pleasant tunnel, on the city side. The making of the railway here interrupted the spring, and it is now sealed up and lost.

The spring belonged to the dean and chapter, as indeed did the whole of St Sidwell's, and they were the first to tap it in order to supply the cathedral chapter with fresh water. This was brought in pipes sunk in trenches all the way from Lions Holt, and into the city through large underground passages. In 1226 the dean granted a third part of the water supply to St Nicholas Priory.

29   St Nicholas Priory Guest Hall

In 1346, we discover, the water was brought underground to an enclosed building in the Cathedral Yard, whence it was taken off in three channels, one for the use of the cathedral clergy, another for the city, and the third for the priory. A big new aqueduct was constructed in 1347-9, and further improvements to the supply made at various times during the 15th century. A grand new conduit was built for the use of the citizens, near the present top of Fore Street, in the year 1441. This was finally taken down in 1770, having stood and supplied the people of Exeter with water (all those without private wells), for more than three hundred years.

Some Medieval People

The medieval citizens of Exeter seem far away and long ago, hardly more than bare names to us now. It is almost impossible to conceive of them as real people very much like ourselves, despite their differences of dress and speech, or that we ourselves will one day be utterly remote and shadowy figures to people walking about in the streets five hundred years hence.

At the most we can catch glimpses of our ancestors in their wills, documents in which men and women reveal something of their true feelings towards the end. Occasionally there are phrases in old wills that make everything in the distant past come alive. There was, for example, John de Shillingford, a canon of Exeter, who was probably born at Shillingford just outside the city, of a well-to-do landed family. He made his will while in London on business, on 26 March in the year 1388. In it he asks to be buried, if it can be conveniently arranged, in the church of Widecombe-in-the-Moor.

There, in the chapel of St Katherine, his mother lay buried, and he wished to be laid beside her, 'so that where I received my first greeting, I may take my last farewell'. In these touching words, written in a house in London in Richard II's reign, the shadowy ghost of Canon Shillingford comes alive for a moment and we realise that he was as human as the rest of us.

Or we may turn to the will of Simon Grendon, 'citizen of Exeter', as he styles himself, dated towards the end of July in the year 1411. He was already a dying man, as his will was proved in St Petrock's church only a month later. After commending his soul to God and to all the saints, he asked to be buried in the cathedral, under the north tower and before the image of the Blessed Mary. A thousand masses were to be said for his soul after his death.

At his funeral there were to be 50 'poor persons' carrying torches, all to be suitably clothed by his executors, and 50 other poor persons without torches, but similarly clothed. After bequests to all the clergy of the cathedral and the city, and to various others like the friars of Exeter and the nuns of Polsloe, he left the large sum of £20 (now equivalent to £50,000 or rather more) for the making of a new conduit to bring water to the Carfax in Exeter, and to other parts of the city. The Carfax was, of course, the cross roads where North Street and South Street met High Street and Fore Street.

There were a few other legacies, and then the residue of his estate was to be devoted to 'the relief of the poor and other charitable purposes' in Exeter. Simon Grendon had actually founded almshouses for ten poor women many years before his death, down in Preston Street, where they remained right down to 1878. In that year they were so dilapidated that they were rebuilt in Grendon Road.

The will of Walter Trote, canon of Exeter and rector of St Kerrian (which stood in North Street until 1878) is also very revealing. There are elaborate arrangements for his funeral in the cathedral, at which six poor men, clad in grey cloaks with grey hoods, were to carry torches weighing 13lb. apiece.

Walter Trote also was a man of compassion. Among his numerous bequests were fourpence apiece to every prisoner in the king's prison in Exeter (this was in the great South Gate of the city and an infamous place it was) and to every prisoner in the Bishop's prison likewise.

30 The Great Conduit in the High Street, at the Carfax.

From some of the wills we get a rough idea of the wealth of the parish clergy in Exeter. Just as today, there were wealthy parsons and poor ones. The rector of St Paul's was worth only £13 17s. 11d. when his estate was valued after his death (roughly about £35,000 now), but the rector of St Petrock, who died a few years later, in 1418, left estate to the value of £210 3s. 3½d. (say about £500,000 or rather more today).

There were, indeed, even poorer clergy than the rector of St Paul's, but it becomes very difficult to trace those with little property in past centuries, and they remain completely lost to us.

When the rector of Holy Trinity died in April 1415 he left, among many other bequests, money to enable 'all his parishioners, old as well as young, to be feasted on the day of his burial', while those who nursed him in his last illness were 'to be remunerated well, and not grudgingly, according to their deserts'.

William Wilford, who made his will at the end of June in the year 1413, was a rich merchant. He had been mayor no fewer than seven times, and had sat for Exeter in four parliaments. He left behind personal estate to the value of £228 6s. 9d. We may regard this as the typical estate of a rich citizen at that date. He had lived in the parish of St Petrock, then and for centuries afterwards one of the richest parishes in the city, and he had much house-property besides.

He, too, left money towards improving the water-supply of the city. Among numerous bequests of the usual kind, he left to William Thorne, his servant, a life interest in one of his shops in the parish of St Pancras. We also discover that he had a half share in a ship—*le Marie* of Exmouth—which may be the very ship in which, ten years earlier, he had raided the coast of Brittany and captured 40 ships laden with oil and wine, a memorable exploit for a mayor of Exeter.

Most of his will is taken up with the disposal of his house-property, and also—as was customary at this time—with many details about the religious observances at his funeral and long afterwards. And finally, from his will, we learn a little about his house near St Petrock's church. It had a hall and chamber, a kitchen, a pantry, and a buttery. This sounds very small, but it was in fact the typical house of a wealthy merchant round about 1400. It had only a ground floor and a first floor, and occupied very little space, probably with a large garden or courtyard behind. It was not until about a hundred years later that space became so valuable in the middle of the city that houses were built up to three, four, and occasionally five, storeys, and that the big gardens were also built over.

The best surviving example of a 15th-century merchant's house in Exeter, and indeed one of the best examples of its kind in England, is the old house which stood at the corner of Edmund Street and Frog Street. It was moved in 1961 to a site opposite St Mary Steps to allow Western Way to be constructed. It has the shop and kitchen on the ground floor, the hall and buttery on the first floor, and the solar above that again. The upper floors were reached by a newel stair going up from the kitchen.

The Labourer and his Wages

The great majority of Exeter people have always, from time immemorial, had to earn their livings by the sweat of their brow. It is usually not difficult to discover something about the more literate or the wealthier citizens, such as merchants or parsons, but about the labouring class it is hard to find any record at all.

Yet it is wrong in any history of the city to say nothing about the majority of the inhabitants, and we do know something at any rate about their wages and conditions of work, and a little about the kind of houses they lived in.

It is possible to set out, for example, the wage rates for the Exeter labourer from 1160 down to 1960, a space of eight hundred years. In 1160 he was getting a penny a day. In 1960 an unskilled labourer in Exeter got about £8 a week, or roughly thirty shillings a day (for a 5½-day week), i.e. more in one day than his ancestor earned in a whole year. But there is, of course, very much more in the story than these simple and rather misleading facts.

The unskilled man who toiled every day at the building of Rougemont Castle, or down below at the building of the cathedral which was going on

31 The house at the corner of Frog Street and Edmund Street before it was moved.

32 The House That Moved illuminated at night in 1981 to commemorate the 20th anniversary of the move.

at the same time, earned one penny a day and worked six days a week if he was lucky. A foot-soldier or a carter got the same rate of pay.

The labouring class as a whole lived in the utmost poverty, in small one-roomed huts probably built of cob or with a simple timber frame, with the very minimum of furniture and utensils. The total value of the goods and chattels of such work-people amounted on an average to about ten shillings, and some had less than this.

We know more about wage-rates in Exeter when the building accounts of the cathedral begin, which is in 1279, and from the receivers' accounts among the city records which begin in 1306 (though this is a solitary account and the series really begins in 1339 and continues almost unbroken for the next five hundred years).

In the closing years of the 13th century, master craftsmen working at the cathedral were getting 2s. 3d. to 2s. 6d. a week, probably 2s. 3d. a week if they had regular employment on a long job, and 5d. a day if employed by the day as most men ordinarily were. The building of a cathedral or a castle, which could keep men regularly employed for month after month and year after year, was exceptional. Most labourers could not reckon on six days' work a week all the year round, far from it.

The assistants to master craftsmen (journeymen) were getting 1s. 8d. to 1s. 10d. a week at the cathedral, and labourers' wages had risen (in a hundred years) to 9d. or 10d. a week, say 1½d. a day. Carters were equivalent to unskilled labourers, or just slightly better, and earned 10½d. a week at this time, bringing stone and timber to the cathedral.

Labourers' wages moved only very slowly under normal conditions, but an account in the city records for 1368-9 shows that their pay had doubled since about 1300. They were getting 3d. to 3½d. a day, or 1s. 8d. a week. Master masons were getting 5d. a day for work at the Guildhall, and journeymen masons 4d. a day. The doubling of labourers' wages had come about since the Black Death of 1349-50, which by killing off perhaps half of the population in some places had brought about a great scarcity of labour generally.

The three men who worked on a cellar at the Guildhall in 1368 (mason, journeyman, and labourer) were there for 15 days. During that time they got their 'nonsch' (lunch) provided, at a total cost of 3d. for the whole period, that is a penny per head for 15 meals: probably bread, cheese, and beer. Two masons working at the East Gate in the same year earned 2s. 9d. a week each, with their beer thrown in at a cost to the city of one penny. These were master craftsmen, earning the equivalent of 5½d. a day.

Wages continued to rise during the rest of the 14th century and the early 15th, for there was still a relative scarcity of labour, both skilled and unskilled. In 1425 a freemason at the cathedral was paid 6d. a day, his assistant 5d. a day, and labourers 4d. All masters seem to have got the same rates, for a master plumber was also paid 6d. a day at this time.

The labouring class was much better off in the 15th century than it had ever been, but it was not exactly a full life. The wage-rates seem ludicrous to us, but against that we must set the low prices of the time. Thus when the Exeter labourer was getting 9d. or 10d. a week round about 1300 a hen cost 1½d. and eggs were thirty or forty a shilling according to the season. A penny also bought three or four pigeons and about two pounds of cheese. If we wish to make comparisons, therefore, we must really work out a day's wages in terms of the food they would buy.

Even then it is very difficult to make satisfactory comparisons as our notions of comfort and of the things we need are completely different today from those of our medieval forebears. One thing is quite certain, that the labourer today is vastly better off than his ancestors of several centuries ago, whatever hardship he may occasionally encounter.

Wages continued to move up slowly. In 1540 labourers picking ivy off the city walls (because ivy could eventually bring down the whole wall) got 5d. a day, but this was probably a cheap rate for a very simple job, and not very arduous, for demolition workers at St Nicholas Priory about the same time were getting 6d. a day.

So, to sum up the labourer's wages at Exeter, assuming he worked a full six-day week, the picture looks like this for the first 400 years:

About 1160   6d. a week.
1284-1300   9d. to 10d. a week.
1368-9   1s. 8d. a week.
1425   2s. a week.
1540-60   3s. a week.

Some Medieval Buildings

We can see a good deal of the history of Exeter in the Middle Ages merely by looking at the buildings which are still standing. A good deal of the 15th century, especially, survives in various parts of Exeter. Some of it is obvious, such as the little red sandstone churches and almshouses like Wynards in Magdalen Street, but much is hidden behind the rather dull and sometimes shabby facades of ordinary shops and houses.

The Norman cathedral had been completed by about the year 1200 and it remained pretty well unchanged until about 1275. In or about that year Bishop Bronescombe began the rebuilding and enlargement which was to take the next eighty or ninety years to complete. Most English cathedrals are an assortment of styles, but Salisbury and Exeter are two notable exceptions. Exeter, completed about 1360-70, is entirely in one style, that of Decorated Gothic architecture. Externally, the cathedral is not impressive, being too low in relation to its width, but internally it is one of the richest and most harmonious interiors in England. Indeed, there is probably no lovelier interior in this country. When Bishop Grandisson came to the See of Exeter in 1327 he wrote to Pope John XXII that 'the Cathedral of Exeter, now half finished, is marvellous in beauty and when completed will surpass every Gothic church in England and France.'

About a hundred years after the cathedral was completed, the little parish churches of the city were nearly all rebuilt in the coarse, red, Heavitree sandstone, so that they are nearly all in the style we know as Perpendicular Gothic. Most of them, however, retain some evidences of the earlier building. St Mary Steps, for example, still has its Norman font, St Mary Arches retains its two Norman arcades (which make it the best surviving Norman church in Devon), and St Stephen still has its 11th-century crypt hidden away beneath the church.

In the 15th century also, we find new almshouses being built. The best of these still survives in Magdalen Street—Wynard's Hospital (1435) built by William Wynard who was recorder of Exeter from 1418 to 1442. He caused this hospital or almshouse to be built for 12 infirm, poor people, and he also caused a chapel to be built for their use, called Trinity Chapel. The almshouses suffered severely in the Civil War and were considerably repaired afterwards. They also underwent restoration in 1863. In spite of all this Wynard's Hospital, with its little cobbled courtyard and well-house, is one of the most evocative pieces of medieval Exeter. It was used for many years by voluntary organisations but the City Council has now sold it for private occupation. The little chapel of St Clare at Livery Dole was also built about the same time as Wynard's, or a trifle earlier. Both this

33 St Mary Arches church: a pre-war view before the roof was blitzed and repaired.

and Wynard's Chapel are typical examples of 15th-century chapels in the red Exeter sandstone.

Amongst the property with which William Wynard endowed his new hospital was the *White Hart Inn* which still stands in South Street. There is good reason to think that before it passed to the hospital it had been Wynard's own house. Much of the existing building on the ground floor is of 15th-century date—some of it may be a little earlier. It was known as the Blue Boar in Wynard's time. The Blue Boar was one of the badges of Richard, Duke of York, the father of King Edward IV. The richly carved ceiling and fireplace in the lower bar of the hotel probably date from Wynard's time and suggest that this was his private parlour.

One or two other famous medieval inns deserve mention, though they no longer survive. The greatest of all the Exeter inns for several centuries was the *New Inn*, which stood in the High Street immediately to the north-east (on the Bedford Street side) of St Stephen's church. The site of the *New Inn* belonged to the dean and chapter, probably given to them in the early 12th century by the bishop, who owned much property in St Stephen's parish. About the year 1445 the dean and chapter built 'the new mansion' with shops in front of it: so we gather from the rent-collector's account a year or two later. One of Mayor Shillingford's many complaints against the cathedral authorities, in his historic battle with them just at this time, was that the shops or stalls of the *New Inn* had encroached forward on to the High Street.

The *New Inn* became the principal inn of the city, at which the most distinguished visitors were lodged. Indeed, the city fathers seem to have taken long leases of it from the dean and chapter, and to have sub-let it to innkeepers. In the receiver's (city treasurer's) accounts for 1461 there is an item: 'four gallons of wine sent to Lord Stafford at the New Ynne 3s. 4d.'

Farther down the High Street, opposite the Guildhall, stood the *Eagle*, formerly the town house of the merchant-family of Wilford; and in South Street, where the Roman Catholic church now stands, was the long-famous *Bear Inn*. This was the town house of the abbots of Tavistock. They seldom visited it, but leased it as an inn. Exeter was a rich and bustling trading city, with a constant influx of merchants, traders and hangers-on, all of whom needed accommodation. The *Bear Inn* is said to have been rebuilt in 1481, and it remained one of the great inns of the city until the early 19th century. Many other inns, big and little, first appear in the 16th century; but the old *Half Moon*, which stood next to the *New Inn* (between it and Bedford Street), did not become an inn (apparently) until the middle of the 17th century.

The shops or stalls in front of the *New Inn* were a typical way of trading in the Middle Ages. A record in the city archives, dated about 1280, speaks for example of 'a shop and solar over' in North Street 'in front of our tenement towards the street'. The earliest shops were generally very small. A lease in January 1336 mentions a shop in High Street only five feet long by four feet wide, and another shop near Broadgate in 1338 was ten feet by six feet.

The city was gradually filling up within the walls. Space was becoming more valuable. It was not that the population was so great but that so much land inside the walls was what we should call 'sterilised'. The cathedral close, the bishop's palace, the castle and its precincts, and the large sites of the monasteries and friaries, between them took up perhaps a third of the area of the walled city and could not be used for ordinary building.

So we get curious little sites being used, like that of the new rectory for St Kerrian's parish in North Street. This was built in the year 1350, next to the church. Building sites were so scarce in this congested little parish that the mayor allowed the rector to block up the end of an old street, rather like a cork in a long-necked bottle. The street was Trichay Street, which used to run from Pancras Lane to North Street about where the wide ramp now leads to the shopping precinct. The name Trichay has been used elsewhere in the precinct. It is odd that the city fathers should have allowed the rector of St Kerrian's to block the street like this, but they reserved to themselves and their successors 'right of entry into the rectory by a key in time of war, or whenever the need or use of the city may demand it'.

A considerable number of 15th-century houses are still to be found in various parts of the city. The best surviving example is the merchant's house already mentioned, moved from the corner of Frog Street and Edmund Street. Now nearly opposite it, at the foot of Stepcote Hill, is another house,

34   Nos. 11-12 West Street.

35   The *Elephant Inn*, North Street *c.*1960.

or rather pair of houses, built about the same date. These are Nos. 11 and 12 West Street. Like the Frog Street house, each had a shop on the ground floor with a kitchen behind. On the first floor was the hall, or principal living room, with perhaps a buttery, and on the floor above was the solar, or principal bedroom. The original plan of these houses is still clearly traceable.

In the High Street, Nos. 46 and 47 form a pair of houses built about 1490-1500. No. 46 (now Thorntons) retains most of its original front, but No.47 (now Orange mobile phones) has been completely disguised by a later façade. It is clear, however, on looking at the backs of both these houses, that they were originally built at the same time. Probably an old site was divided into two in order to do this. These also were the houses of well-to-do merchants. It is almost invariably merchants' houses which survive because they were better built to start with. The houses of the craftsmen and artisans and the working class generally all fell down or were swept away centuries ago.

Another 15th-century house stands at the corner of St Martin's Lane and Catherine Street. It carries the date 1450, but the authority for this date does not seem to be known. Lastly, in North Street, an interesting little group of late 15th-century houses survived until the Guildhall shopping precinct was built in the 1970s. The age of the houses was not apparent from the outside. Messrs. Mansfield (antique dealers) was a good example internally of a 15th-century dwelling house of a particularly rich merchant, though much altered. Much of the original timbering of the fine hall-roof was still clearly visible. When these were built, North Street was one of the four chief streets of the city and was inhabited for the most part by well-to-do people. Immediately below Messrs. Mansfield was the *Elephant Inn*, which seems to have been rebuilt in the 17th century, and below that again Nos. 35 and 36, undistinguished though they appeared, proved to be, after internal examination, houses of late 15th-century date.

36 House on the corner of St Martin's Lane.

Medieval Sanitation

Only the better-class houses had their own sanitary arrangements: most people had none. When the daughter of Nicholas Holeman, an Exeter mason, married Henry Stubard of St Giles in the Wood in 1345, the girl's parents granted to their new son-in-law 'half the solar with a certain latrine [*cloaca*] in the same, which is situated beyond the high table of the hall in our house' in South Street, together with a stable. Evidently the newly-married pair were to live with her parents and to share the solar or sitting-room.

Another example occurs in a lease by the prior of St Nicholas to John Copleston in September 1401. This was part of a larger house called 'Sullyes Inn' in Paul Street, and consisted of two rooms (probably a hall and solar), a latrine, a stable, and a cellar.

When much of Exeter was burnt by the Germans in May 1942, various medieval buildings were revealed which had hitherto been hidden by later additions. One of these was a 14th-century house in Milk Street. Here the garderobe (the polite word for it in the Middle Ages) was discovered in the front room (solar) of the house, in the thickness of one of the walls. It was entered through a sort of cupboard-door in the wall. A seat was placed across a shaft. This shaft, which formed a wide buttress in the wall on to the street, presumably went down into a cess-pit which could be cleared out from time to time from the street. It seems to have been the general medieval arrangement to have the garderobe opening directly off the sitting-room, not a very salubrious idea but better than nothing at all.

How did other people manage—those whose houses did not contain any such private arrangements? Most people in the medieval city probably had small gardens or yards attached to their houses and these would be put to sanitary (or rather, insanitary) uses. Probably also there were many people not above using the streets and lanes on dark nights, though it would be a punishable offence if they were caught.

37 Toilets on the leat. A photograph from *c.*1970 shows the Lower Leat along Commercial Road below Horse Pool. On the left is the side of Tremlett's tannery.

The city fathers had provided 'common latrines' before 1467.* These stood over one of the mill-leats in the lower part of the town, in all probability the leat near Horsepool Bridge in Edmund Street. There seems to have been something similar on the old Exe Bridge, for Jenkins, in his *History of Exeter*, says that there was an open space in the centre of the bridge 'where there was a door-way and a flight of steps that led to a long vaulted room, commonly called the Pixey or Fairy House'. This is all he says about it, but its purpose seems clear enough.

It is probable that the stream that flowed on the south-east side of the city, well outside the walls, was used from time immemorial as an open sewer. From Saxon times onwards it was always called Shitbrook—the meaning is obvious—but later generations have dropped this coarse Saxon name. The stream itself, which rose near St Ann's chapel at the top of Sidwell Street, flowed down what is now Clifton Road, under the Triangle, and down the steep-sided valley behind Denmark Road to join the Exe near the *Port Royal Inn*. It was covered in and adapted as a storm sewer during the 1840s. Gradually its deep valley has been filled in, too, and soon its course will be completely forgotten. It was possibly not as offensive as it sounds in early days, for it had a steep fall to the river and even now rises and falls very rapidly after rain. The swift current after a rain-storm periodically swept it fresh and clean, and the city was, after all, not very large.

* In London, Queen Maud provided 'a necessary house at Queenhithe for the common use of the citizens' in the early part of the 12th century. These were probably the first public conveniences to be established in England.

The Magdalen Hospital

Indeed, the brook could not have been offensive except in spells of dry weather for the earliest 'hospital' in Exeter was built right beside it. This was the Hospital of St Mary Magdalene for lepers, one of the oldest leper hospitals in England. The oldest of these hospitals was founded at Canterbury in 1096. That at Exeter is first recorded in the time of Bishop Bartholomew (1161-84) but it was old even then. We may assume that it goes back to about 1100, and that it was founded by one of the early bishops of Exeter as the warden of the hospital was appointed by the bishop.

Even at that date it was clearly understood that lepers had to be carefully isolated from inhabited places. The so-called 'leper windows' in parish churches are nothing of the sort: lepers were never allowed to wander about freely as this theory implies. At Exeter the hospital was built on the further bank of the Shitbrook, close to the present Magdalen Road, and half a mile outside the South Gate of the city.

In the year 1244 the city took over the patronage and running of the hospital from the bishop, in exchange for their patronage of St John's Hospital. Among the rules then laid down it was ordered that none of the 13 inmates should cross the bridge outside the hospital gate without the warden's special permission. Anyone disobeying this order was put into the stocks and given only bread and water for a day. For abusing the warden the penalty was bread and water, and the stocks for 12 days, and for striking another inmate 30 days of bread and water in the stocks.

One mayor of the city—Richard Orenge (1454)—contracted leprosy and retired into the hospital. He died there in 1458 and was buried in the chapel which stood near by. The other well-known hospital in Exeter, for poor men and women—the first true almshouse in the city—was St John's Hospital, founded in all probability some time in the third quarter of the 12th century (1150-75) to judge by the Norman arcade shown in an old drawing of the ruins. As early as 1289 eight children were being boarded and educated in the hospital.

The Courtenays and the River

The relations between the city and the cathedral authorities were frequently strained in the Middle Ages. Another constant source of friction, and later of real harm to the city, was its peculiar situation in relation to the earls of Devon. The jurisdiction of the city on the southern side ceased at the city walls. Beneath the walls in Roman times had been a marsh merging into the river. But when this marsh was reclaimed by the making of leats (as already described) the valuable new land so created—Exe Island—belonged to the earls of Devon. By the 13th century, therefore, the earls were in a position to control the river and to interfere seriously with the city's sea-borne trade.

For a long time the Courtenays, to whom the earldom of Devon eventually came, were content to develop their rich industrial property with all its mills and industries, and a growing population that needed housing. But by the early days of the 14th century they began to interfere with the navigation of the river. Since they owned the manor of Topsham they stood to gain a large revenue if they could force all Exeter-bound ships to discharge their cargoes at Topsham quay instead of Exeter. The traditional story is that Isabella de Fortibus, countess of Devon in her own right, made two weirs across the river, leaving a 30-foot gap between them so that shipping could pass up to Exeter, for the purpose of driving a new mill built within her manor of Topsham. This was in the year 1284, and it was this weir that gave its name to the village of Countess Wear. But Hugh de Courtenay, who succeeded to the title and possessions of Isabella, stopped up the 30-foot gap (about the year 1311) and so prevented ships and boats from reaching the city at all. They were forced to unload at the earl's new quay at Topsham, and to store their cargoes in his cellars, to his great benefit.

There are discrepancies in the traditional story, but it is broadly true that the river was blocked by the Courtenays. From then onwards the city and the Courtenays were constantly at loggerheads. The rich salmon fishery of the city was injured, the tide no longer came up to Exeter as it used to do, the merchants' cellars were empty. One interesting fact put forward by the city in a record of 1317 was that 'the Island of Exe was common, and served the city' and that sand deposited there by high tides had always been common property for the citizens, who had fetched it from time to time for the repair of their houses and other buildings. Similarly the fishing in the river had always been free for all. But now Hugh Courtenay, earl of Devon, had appropriated the fishing and the sand, and sold both on hard terms.

Petition after petition went up from the city to various kings, but little or nothing seems to have been done. In the 15th century, especially, the Courtenays were a law unto themselves, and there was continual friction between them and the city because of the unfortunate geographical accident which had given them a foothold between the city walls and the river. When, in the year 1538, the head of the Courtenays—Henry, marquis of Exeter—was attainted and executed for an alleged conspiracy against the king (Henry VIII), a great burden was lifted from the city fathers. Courtenay's lands were confiscated by the Crown, and their influence ceased abruptly. In December 1550 the age-old problem of Exe Island was settled, when Edward VI gave it to the city as a recognition of their defence against the Catholic rebels in the preceding year.

Within two years of the Courtenays' downfall, too, the city fathers set to work to reopen the river in some way to navigation. They obtained an act of parliament in 1540 for this purpose and made various attempts to solve the problem by clearing the river. All these failed, and in 1563 it was decided that a canal, by-passing the obstacles, was the only solution.

CHAPTER FIVE

Exeter People in the Sixteenth Century

Wealth and Poverty

IN THE FIRST QUARTER of the 16th century Exeter was still one of the largest and richest towns in England. London towered over all other towns, but in the provinces the only towns that exceeded Exeter in size were Norwich, Bristol, and Newcastle. In wealth Exeter stood fifth in the provinces.

There were probably about 8,000 people living in the city and suburbs at this time (the reign of Henry VIII), of whom the great majority were poor or very poor. In the year 1522, for example, nearly two adults in every five were assessed at nil in the records. They lived in rented cottages with very little furniture and possessed only the tools of their trade and the clothes they stood up in. They had literally nothing that could be taxed. Of the remaining 5,000 people, just about one-half were assessed on 'wages', which were reckoned for tax purposes at only twenty to forty shillings a year.

At the other end of the social scale, 60 men were assessed on personal estate to the value of £40 or more (equivalent to about £100,000 today), and of these a half were reckoned to be worth £100 or more—that is, £250,000 or more in modern values. The richest man in Exeter (William Crugge) had died just before this assessment, but his widow and eldest son appear in it. Together they are assessed at £766 13s. 4d. representing a fortune (in personal estate alone) of nearly £2,000,000. Other rich men reckoned to be worth over £500,000 (in modern values), were William Hurst, John Brycknoll, Robert Buller, John Bradmore, John Blackaller, Richard Androwe, Gilbert Kirk, Henry Hamlyn, William Periam, Thomas Hodge, and Thomas Herrys. The richest parishes all lay in the heart of the city. Some of them are very poor today, like St Mary Arches and St Olave.

To put it in another way, there were about 1,500 adults in the city who attracted the attention of the tax authorities. Of these, about 550 turned out to be worth nothing, so leaving 956 people to be taxed. Of this total, 458 were assessed on wages or goods to the annual value of 20s. to 40s. These are the poor, the labouring class; and together with those too poor to be taxed at all they made up just about two-thirds of the population. A large proportion of the untaxable consisted of old men no longer capable of work, poor widows, and men incapable of doing an ordinary job.

Above this mass of poor families—two in every three in the city, living at a level that would not be tolerated today—stood the craftsman and shopkeeper class (nearly one-third of the taxed population) assessed at goods to the value of £2 to £10. Above £10 we may say we reach the comfortable level—175 assessments—shading off into the rich merchant class already mentioned whose personal fortunes generally ranged between £100 and £300 at that date.

These figures are only a rough guide to the wealth of different social classes but they give us a fair idea of the widespread poverty of the time, tempered by acts of private charity, and of the very unequal distribution of wealth even four hundred or more years ago.

For the greater part of the population we have indeed some notion of their weekly income. When the Exeter magistrates fixed maximum wage-rates in 1564, labourers and apprentices in the building trades were to get 6d. a day, journeymen 8d., and master-craftsmen (mason, carpenter, joiner, plasterer, slater, tiler, thatcher, and plumber) 10d. a day. Farm-labourers also got 6d. a day, rising to 8d. a day between March and September. An unmarried woman servant, living in, got 16s. a year up to 24 years of age (with 5s. for her clothing allowance) rising to 20s. a year at 24 years and upwards, with 6s. 8d. for clothing.

No official change was made in these rates of wages as late as 1588, though the cost of living rose steadily all through the second half of the 16th century. But by the 1620s labourers' wages had doubled (to 1s. a day) with the same for journeymen craftsmen, and 1s. 2d. a day for master-craftsmen.

In a full week's work, then, the Exeter labourer could get 3s. a week in the middle decades of the century, and 6s. a week by the 1620s. He was no better off in the latter years as the cost of living had also at least doubled. But in the building trades especially labourers and craftsmen could not reckon on 52 weeks' work a year, and six days a week. Taking the year as a whole, bad weather with fine, good employment with bad, it is likely that the full wage of 3s. a week in, say, 1550, was nearer an average of 2s. to 2s. 6d. all the year round. We do not know what rents were paid by the wage-earning class for the hovels they lived in, but at Coventry, a very similar city to Exeter at this date, rents of 5s. to 10s. a year were the usual level for working-class houses. Some labourers paid as little as 2s. to 3s. a year. The average labourer paid 5s. a year. A Coventry physician paid 26s. 8d. a year, roughly the equivalent of 6d. a week, a fishmonger and a mercer 50s. a year, butchers from 10s. to 53s. 4d. So 1s. a week rent provided a decent house for a superior tradesman. These figures undoubtedly applied also to a city like Exeter. Such small rents were not paid weekly, but probably quarterly.

Some Exeter Mayors

In the latter part of the 16th century John Hooker, the city chamberlain, kept a Commonplace Book and in this he wrote brief character sketches of several of the mayors. With these and a few other details we can gather from other records, we can get some idea, partial though it is, of what some of the 16th-century mayors were like as persons.

The first one of whom we have any real knowledge is William Crugge, or Crudge. He was mayor four times between 1506 and 1518 and when he died in 1520 he was the wealthiest merchant in Exeter. Hooker tells us that he was at first a tanner living in Exe Island. He was maimed in a violent quarrel, sued his aggressor at law, and recovered such damages that by shrewd use of the money he became a rich merchant, so enabling his descendants to live as gentlemen. Hooker goes on: 'He was somewhat self-willed and not easily to be removed from the opinion which he had formed, which was an occasion sometimes of some disliking between him and his brethren.' He was, however, very diligent in public service and spent freely when he thought it necessary for the good of the community. For many years William Crugge continued to live in Exe Island in the parish of St Mary Steps, but in 1498 he moved up into the parish of St Kerrian and there he lived for the last twenty years or so of his life in a large 'mansion house' standing next to St Kerrian's church. The site of his house is now occupied by Woolworth's side window in North Street.

As a rich trading city, Exeter drew able young men from all parts of the country to make their fortunes, and a surprising number of our 16th-century mayors actually came in from elsewhere. John Buckenam, for example, who was mayor in 1509 and 1516, was born in Suffolk. His father was a gentleman in that county, but John, being a younger brother, had no prospects at home and was sent to Exeter and trained as a merchant and eventually became very rich. Hooker says he 'behaved himself in great wisdom and uprightness, for which he was greatly reverenced and esteemed, and so much the more that he kept a very good house and a liberal hospitality'. He had no children and he left his fortune to a nephew, William Buckenam, who became mayor in 1541 but was not as good a man as his uncle.

Geoffrey Lewis, who became mayor in 1519, had been born in Wales but came to Exeter and prospered as a merchant tailor. Hooker says he was 'a wise man and very provident in all his doings. He was very good to the poor and much affected to the Lazar House of the Maudlyn over whom he was made warden and so continued many years until his dying day'. This, of course, was the leper hospital of St Mary Magdalene.

John Nosworthy, who became mayor in 1521, is also described as 'a very wise and a learned man, professing the laws of this realm'. Exeter seems to have been fortunate in its 16th-century mayors. Mr Nosworthy, we are told, governed the city so well that there had been no better mayor before or since. He lost all his private practice as a lawyer and gave himself entirely to public service. Among other things, he reformed many abuses in the mayor's court and the provost's court, two of Exeter's ancient courts of law, and he also had made a great chest for the safekeeping of the city records. These had, until now, been very carelessly looked after, with no proper accommodation for them so that (as Izacke tells us) most of the records from the Norman Conquest down to the time of Henry III had been lost. What remains to us today is the finest collection of civic records outside the city of London, but it is evident that we have also lost much that would have been of the greatest value for writing the history of the city in the early Middle Ages.

We are also told about Mr John Nosworthy that there was a great scarcity of corn, and therefore of bread, during his mayoralty in the late spring of 1522. Since bread was the great standby for the mass of the population at this time, a shortage of corn literally meant a famine, and like other mayors of that time, Mr Nosworthy had to deal with the situation out of his own pocket. He bought up a large store of corn and distributed it to the poor 'which got him the love of the people all the days of his life thereafter'.

The next mayor after Mr Nosworthy was Mr Richard Duke. He too was a gentleman born, but being a younger brother, again with no prospects of inheriting any family property, he was trained as a lawyer. Hooker says 'he was well learned and practiced and did much good to the commonwealth of this city'. We are also told that he was a great personal friend of John Nosworthy. During his mayoralty he reformed the ale-houses and tippling houses of the city. He found that many evils arose from these places 'such as drunkenness and whoredom' and he introduced a system whereby everyone who kept an ale-house or a common tavern should enter into recognisances for the good behaviour of their houses.

38   Nos. 225-6 High Street, Elizabethan merchants' houses from 1576 (from a drawing made in 1827).

We happen to know where Mr Duke lived in Exeter. It was in the large 'mansion house' which stood at the corner of Gandy Street and High Street. This property is now occupied by Top Shop, and was formerly the offices of the old *Devon & Exeter Gazette*. Before that it was for many generations, and indeed centuries, a fine town house occupied for the most part by rich merchants. Richard Duke took a lease of this house from the dean and chapter on 20 March 1502, and there he lived until his death. It is worth remarking that it was in this house that the famous Sir Thomas Bodley was born, the founder of the Bodleian Library at Oxford. He was the son of John Bodley, merchant of this city, who took a lease of the house from the dean and chapter on 9 December 1543, for a term of 70 years. And here, on 2 March 1545, Thomas Bodley was born. In the same house, too,

Mayor Shillingford had written some of his famous letters in the 1440s. The house was rebuilt in 1585 by George Smith, a rich Elizabethan merchant.

The Reformation

It is not easy to explain briefly the Reformation and the form it took in Exeter. I may begin perhaps with the simplified statement I have made elsewhere:*

> England today is mainly a Protestant country, though there is a strong Roman Catholic minority. Before the time of Henry VIII England was a Catholic country. During the 16th century the national religion changed from Catholic to Protestant; but this change was not accomplished without a terrible and bitter struggle in which the people of Devon played a leading part.

In the early 16th century the city of Exeter, dominated by its cathedral, was full of parish churches, chapels, monastic houses, hospitals, and friaries. There were 19 parish churches, containing many chantry chapels; and scattered about the city, either inside the walls or just outside them, were a number of little medieval chapels like that at Livery Dole, or Wynard's, or St Roche's in Coombe Street, and several others. Of monasteries there were only two, both rather small. St Nicholas's Priory in the heart of the city, was a small Benedictine house, and about a mile or so outside the East Gate of the city was Polsloe Priory, which contained 14 nuns at the time of its dissolution in 1538. St James' Priory, beside the river and well below the city, had been dissolved as an alien Priory many years earlier and its revenues transferred to King's College, Cambridge. Cowick Priory, too, had been dissolved long before. Of the hospitals, the most important was St John's Hospital just inside the East Gate, which was inhabited by a prior and three brethren at the Dissolution. It also contained 13 paupers and nine students of grammar. There were two friaries, the Dominican, which stood where Bedford Street now is, and the Franciscan, which stood well outside the South Gate near the street still known as The Friars.

The first sign of the impending violence that the Reformation was to bring was the burning of Thomas Benet in 1531. He was a schoolmaster in Exeter and an early reformer. He posted on the cathedral doors anonymous attacks on Catholic doctrines, but his son was detected in the act early one morning. Benet was brought before the diocesan authorities and some of the city magistrates, who examined him as to his beliefs. Since he refused to recant he was burnt alive at Livery Dole, just outside the city boundaries, the first of the two Protestant martyrs in Devon.

The next signs of violent feeling appeared in 1535 when the King's commissioners arrived in the West to examine the affairs of all the lesser religious houses. In the summer of that year they reached Exeter and began work at St Nicholas's Priory. After looking this over, they went to dinner having ordered a workman, while they were away, to pull down the rood

---

* In *Devon and Its People*, p. 76. For the best account of the Reformation in Exeter, see Chapter 8 of MacCaffrey's *Exeter 1540-1640*, on which my pages here are largely based.

loft in the Priory Church. This was a swift and extremely tactless order. Before they returned from their dinner, certain good Catholic women, hearing of the outrage, and determining to put a stop to it, came to the church. The door was fastened but they broke it open and finding the workman pulling down the rood loft they attacked him and hurled stones at him. He fled into the church tower for refuge, but they pursued him so eagerly that he was forced to jump out of a window to save himself. He barely escaped breaking his neck, and indeed broke one of his ribs. John Blackaller, one of the City aldermen, being advised of what was going on, went with all speed to the monastery, thinking to pacify the women. But 'they were plain with him, and the foresaid Elizabeth Glanfield gave him a blow and sent him packing'. Next the mayor turned up. He was unwilling that the king's commissioners should get to hear of this trouble; but when he arrived the women had locked themselves in the church and put themselves in readiness to stand a siege. The mayor and his officers managed to break into the church, apprehended the women, and took them all into custody. By this time the king's commissioners had to be told what was going on. They thanked the mayor for his diligence in suppressing the disturbance, but before they left Exeter they besought him to release the women from custody.

No amount of Catholic opposition, however, sufficed to prevent the dissolution of the monasteries and other religious foundations in the city. St Nicholas's Priory was the first to go in 1536. Polsloe Priory managed to postpone the evil day for a couple more years, but it, too, went in 1538, in the same year as the two friaries. Then began the scramble for the properties which had belonged to these ancient foundations. The city fathers were particularly anxious that no magnate should acquire an undue amount of property in or near the city. They had suffered too much in the past from the proximity of the Courtenays right outside their walls; and so, when the spoils were sold off, we find that the merchants and other rich men of the city obtained most of what was going.

For the next few years there was comparative quiet, but then in the summer of 1549 came the uprising of the Devon and Cornish peasantry, led by several of the gentry, which is generally known as the Prayerbook Rebellion. The Catholic rebels marched upon the City of Exeter, the capture of which they regarded as essential to their success. They began to lay siege to the city on 2 July hoping that the considerable Catholic party inside the walls would open the gates to them. Many of the senior citizens were true Catholics, but their sense of civic responsibility, and perhaps their fear of a general pillage of the merchant houses and shops by the rebels, led them to keep the gates shut. At last, after five weeks of siege and great suffering within the city, the mercenary army of John, Lord Russell, a good Protestant and one of the greatest receivers of monastic spoils in England, relieved the city and the rebellion was over. The vicar of St Thomas was hanged from his own church tower by the brutal Russell.

The reformers enjoyed a brief reign of authority under the new bishop, Miles Coverdale, but then, in July 1553, came the news that Mary had succeeded to the throne. Coverdale was actually preaching in the cathedral when the news came. We are told that the whole congregation, except a few, trooped out, and shortly afterwards Bishop Coverdale left the country. There was a strong Catholic party in the city all through Mary's reign. But then in 1558 the new Queen Elizabeth ascended the throne and once more the Catholics were on the run. We do not know all that happened in these years of change and counter-change, and it took perhaps a whole generation to eradicate Catholic feeling in the city. Probably this was accomplished mainly through the schools, in which the young were suitably indoctrinated with the new religion, and through the pulpits of the parish churches which undermined the older generation slowly. By the end of the century Exeter was a safely Protestant city.

Some Old By-Laws

One of the many ways in which we can get the flavour of the past is by looking at the regulations made from time to time by the city fathers. They often give us that detail which brings back the past more vividly than any large-scale piece of history like a battle or a coronation. Many of us feel there are far too many dogs in the city today, creatures of anti-social habits who have no place in a large built-up area. Our forefathers thought the same at times and with considerable reason. They regarded dogs as carriers of infection in an age when plague could break out suddenly and ravage a whole town. The mayor in 1423 put it like this:

> For as much as great damages do grow within this city as well in the night times and especially in the infectious times of sickness by keeping of dogs within this City, which do not only in the night times bark and fight in the streets to the annoyance of people in their beds but also do in the day time run from house to house where the sickness is, therefore no man shall henceforth keep any dog or dogs within this city at any time.

Anyone keeping a dog was fined 12d. for every such animal (roughly £125 today) and watchmen finding any dogs were empowered to kill them at once. A regulation like this would cause a revolution today. In 1509 the regulation was modified but was still severe: no one was allowed to have a dog running about the streets, under a penalty of a fine of 4d. (about £50 today). For some curious reason, not explained in the regulations, spaniels were excepted from these prohibitions.

There were several regulations relating to brewers. Our forefathers drank ale until about the time of Henry VIII when beer was introduced into Exeter. Beer-drinking was brought back to England from the Low Countries in the early 15th century, but it took about a hundred years to reach Exeter. From then onwards the beer-brewers grew rapidly at the expense of the ale-brewers; brewing became a flourishing industry in Exeter during the reign of Queen Elizabeth I. Apparently die brewers needed a lot of watching. They were up to every trick. The city council became so exasperated in the early weeks of the year 1563 that at their meeting on 1 February they said categorically that the mayor should consult with the brewers who were 'to brew henceforth a more wholesome drink, or else order to be taken for the setting up of a common brewhouse'. In other words, unless the brewers would toe the line and produce good beer the city would set up its own brewery and supplant them. No more is heard of this threat, but it is a striking illustration of the swift, sharp methods of the time.

The mayor and council in former times had much greater dictatorial powers than they have today. In 1566 the council fixed the maximum price of rabbits at 10d. a pair (best quality) with the skin reserved to the seller. There was a 40s. fine (today equivalent to £2,500) for selling above this maximum price.

The council meeting on 13 December 1557 passed an excellent resolution for their own business. 'In order that all things should be done in a decent, good, and seemly manner in the council chamber when the mayor and Twenty Four are assembled there' it was agreed that 'if any one of the Twenty Four offer and mind to speak on any matter' he shall do so without interruption from anyone else—except that 'if the mayor for the time being shall think his talk to be too tedious, too long, or to small effect' he shall be fined 12d. (about £150 today) by the mayor for every such offence. One wonders if this admirable order was ever observed: how splendid for a chairman to be able to fine a bore £150 on the spot and make him sit down forthwith!

One of the old customs which might well be revived today, with the endless slaughter on the roads, is that of the deodand. Anything which caused the death of a human being was forfeited (literally, 'given to God'). Deodands were abolished in 1846, but might well be revived so as to enable motor cars to be forfeited in cases where it is proved they have caused the death of a human being. This penalty would do more to diminish the appalling slaughter than any other measure: in this respect, as in so many others, our ancestors were far more intelligent than we are.

In 1541 a young child called Thomas Hunt, standing near the wheel of a horse mill which Nicholas Reeve, a brewer, had built, was swept into the cog-wheel and torn to pieces. At the inquest it was found that the wheel was the cause of the child's death, whereupon the mill was immediately pulled down and the horse forfeited to the city as a deodand. This was a severe penalty, but the plain truth is that our forefathers valued human life above personal property, whereas we unfortunately do not. Drunken or aggressive motorists would disappear in a few months if they knew that the penalty on conviction was the forfeiture of their precious car.

Fire was a very great risk in a crowded old city. Most houses were timber-framed, with much lath and plaster. Thatched roofs were prohibited inside the city walls, but outside, in streets like Sidwell Street and Paris Street, nearly every cottage was thatched. The penalties for allowing one's house to catch fire, or even a chimney, were therefore severe. In 1583 the penalty for a house-fire was 20s. (say £1,000 today) and a chimney on fire meant a fine of 6s. 8d. (say £350 today). In the richer parts of the city men built their houses with massive stone party-walls. Several of these can still be seen to this day where 15th- and 16th-century houses survive, as for example between Nos. 40 and 41 High Street, or in the medieval houses on Stepcote Hill.

But these 'fire breaks' did not help most of the city, and early in 1559 we find the council taking the first elementary steps to provide fire-fighting equipment. A special rate was levied to raise money for the purchase of four dozen leather buckets. These were to be hung in various convenient places, in readiness for use. Also purchased were 12 ladders and four iron crooks for pulling down burning thatch from roofs.

The city acquired its fire-engine nearly seventy years later, in 1626. This veteran, which still survives, had no wheels but was carried like a sedan chair by means of poles thrust through iron sockets in the sides. It consisted of a leather tank in the middle and a rudimentary pumping apparatus. Arrived at the fire, or near it, leather buckets were filled from the nearest conduit and emptied into the tank, from which water was pumped through a hose directed by a fireman standing on the engine. There could have been few fires on which it made much impression. Some of the buckets were used for beer for the firemen, for pumping was thirsty work. It was said in later years that the larger buckets contained beer and the smaller ones water.

Sanitation also became a pressing problem as the city filled up inside the walls and streets became more congested. There were already common latrines over one of the leats outside the West Gate in the 15th century, as we have seen. But the time came when these were not enough. Whole areas of the city had no sanitary conveniences at all. So on 4 November 1568 the city council agreed that 'there shall be three Common Jakes or Widraughtes made within this city, viz, one in Friernhay, and one at the Town Wall in St Paul's parish, and the third about the Watergate'. The whereabouts of these common 'houses of office' as they were often called, is not exactly known today, except that in Friernhay, which lay at the Snail Tower. We know this because in 1665 the council resolved to re-erect these houses of office, which had presumably fallen into disuse for some reason. It will be noticed that apart from that at the Watergate, these necessary places were not near any water. Presumably they discharged by deep shafts into the ground below the walls.

Each year the newly installed mayor publicly proclaimed, on entry into office, the duties of citizens.

39 Bartholomew Terrace, site of Snayle Tower.

Most people could not read and a loud voice had to serve the general purpose
of telling people what their duties and obligations were. The proclamation
was a long one, and I select here only a few of the social regulations, so
to speak. No householder was to give lodging to any person for more than
one night without knowing who he was or where he came from. Nor was
any householder allowed to let his house to any other person whatsoever
without first informing the mayor or the alderman of his ward, whose
consent was to be obtained.

It was strictly forbidden to throw any household filth into the street, or
any water—whether dirty or clean—out of the window to the annoyance
of passers-by. Householders having a house, garden, or stable in the city
or suburbs were required to sweep and cleanse the street before their
properties once a week. Nor were they to sweep the rubbish into a corner
and especially not into 'the cannells' (that is, the gutters in the middle of
the street, such as we still see on Stepcote Hill). Exeter householders no
longer have to perform this duty, but it is still a common sight in small
German towns to see housewives or servants sweeping and washing down
the street in front of their houses on Saturday afternoons, so as to leave the
whole town clean and sweet for Sunday. If you want to see what Exeter
looked like in the 16th and 17th centuries, and how townspeople lived and
worked and performed their social duties, you can see it perfectly mirrored
in any little walled town in Southern Germany today, smells and all.

Nobody was to walk about the streets on dark nights 'after the last
bell named the bowe bell' had been rung, at nine o'clock in the evening,
unless he carried a light with him. And every householder after dark had
to close and make fast his front door 'and to keep all good rule, order, and
tranquillity'.

The First Tennis Courts

A recently published volume of the State Papers (Patent Rolls) has yielded
an interesting piece of information about the earliest tennis courts in
Exeter. On 26 February 1565 the Queen granted a licence to Richard Prowze
of Exeter, draper, and John Prowze, his eldest son, to keep in Exeter and
the suburbs thereof a 'tenys playe' and a garden with bowling alleys for the
recreation of gentlemen and other fit persons of the better sort of citizens
(these are the actual words of the licence) but excluding 'others of the infe-
rior sort, servants, idle and masterless persons and apprentices'. If any of the
latter class were admitted, the licence would be cancelled upon information
being given to two justices of the peace of the county or to the mayor or
other head officers of the city. So the game of tennis is over four hundred
years old in the city. It is interesting to note that some tennis clubs at least
(though not all) remain the last strongholds of an old-fashioned suburban
snobbery which one would have thought incredible in the second half of
the 20th century. It appears to go back to the very beginnings of the game;
but that is no particular reason for hanging on to it.

Exeter in 1587

The earliest map of Exeter, by Hogenberg, sometimes known as Hooker's map, gives us an interesting picture of the city as it was in Elizabethan days (see overleaf). It is really a combination of a map and a bird's-eye view. Where it can be tested it is surprisingly accurate in its details though not, of course, drawn to scale. It shows Exeter with its walls and towers still complete, and with small suburbs outside each of the four main gates.

To take the river first, the map shows only two weirs—Callabere Weir (now Blackaller Weir) and St Leonard's Weir (now Trews Weir). Trews Weir had been made in 1564 when the construction of the canal was started. Callabere Weir is somewhat older. It certainly existed in 1550 but how long before that we do not know. The map shows men fishing for salmon with a large net immediately below the weir.

Near the weir we find the Bonhay Mills and the large open space fronting the river all the way down to Exe Bridge, which was known as Bonhay and was a favourite walk of the citizens for centuries. Trees lined the river-bank, and it must have been one of the most attractive parts of old Exeter.

The old Exe Bridge is clearly shown, together with all the mill leats and the island called 'the Shellye'. 'The Keye' is shown fronting the leat where it rejoins the river. It was of very limited length. Not until the late 17th century was it extended down-river to the bottom of Colleton Buildings where it ends today, in 1960 grass-grown and deserted except by fishermen on Sunday mornings. A crane is shown on Hogenberg's map, on the end of the quay, and near it the 'Crane Seller'. Behind the quay is shown the Watergate, a new gate in the city wall, making five in all. Farther down river, the 'New Haven' is shown, with ships entering and leaving. This is the canal, which had been opened for traffic just 20 years earlier.

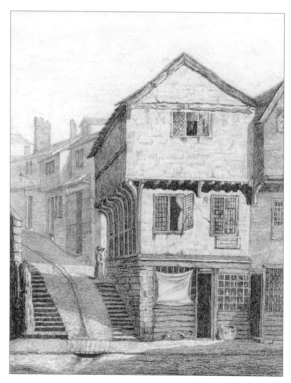

All these features were quite new. They represent the determined efforts of the city fathers, after the downfall of the Courtenays in 1538, to restore Exeter's position as a sea-port to which shipping could once more come. Their attempts in the 1540s to clear the river of the medieval weirs had failed, and after much discussion it was decided to cut a canal around them and so

40 Stepcote Hill drawn by John Gendall in 1834.

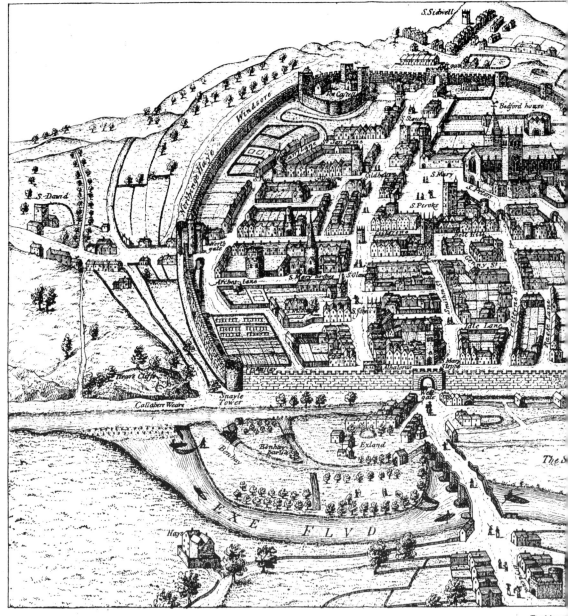

TOWNSEN

41 A 19th-century copy of Hooker's map of 1587.

bypass them. Work was begun on the canal in February 1564, and it was opened to shipping in the autumn of 1566. Constructed under the supervision of John Trew, it was the first canal in England to use the device of the pound-lock. This canal was much shorter than the present one. It was 3,120 yards long and re-entered the Exe at Matford Brook, just above the present Countess Wear bridge. It was 16 feet wide, three feet deep, and took vessels up to sixteen tons. For various reasons it proved to

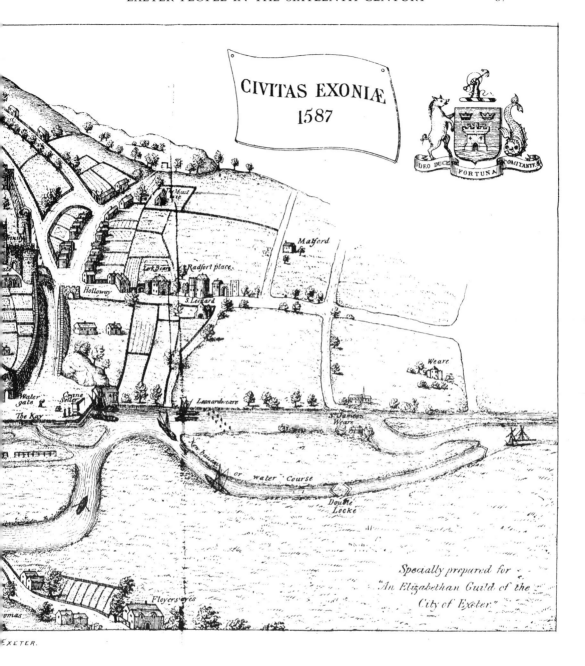

CIVITAS EXONIÆ
1587

be unsatisfactory, but at least it was a start in the long struggle to re-open Exeter as a port.

While the canal was under construction, the Chamber (the city council of the time) also built a new quay, and made a new gate through the city walls to give access to it. At their meeting on 25 July 1565, they agreed that 'a convenient place for a wharf or key shall be without the Watergate of the city'. This was duly built, 'all of ashlar-work', 150 feet long and 80 feet

42 The Exeter Ship Canal, with the city in the background, from a drawing made about 1850.

wide, and a crane erected upon it for loading and unloading. The original Elizabethan quay can still be seen behind the fish-cellars, running from Quay Bridge (over the leat) to the point where the leat enters the river.

At their meeting in July 1565 the Chamber decided to make a gate through the walls, and a night watchman was appointed until the work was completed. By January 1566 the new gate was finished and a porter appointed. He was directed to lock the gate every night at dusk and to bring the keys to the mayor every evening. It was pulled down in 1815. The 'Watergate' mentioned in a 15th-century document probably refers to an opening where the Coombe stream ran out through the city wall. There was no gate at this corner of the walls before the Quay Gate was built.

Returning now to Hogenberg's map, outside the South Gate Magdalen Street is clearly shown running as far as the Magdalen leper hospital. Holloway Street is shown with a castellated medieval mansion at the foot of it. This was Larkbeare, a big house which stood where Roberts Road now joins Holloway Street. Only its truncated central part still stands. A little further on, on the hill known as St Leonard's Down, Radford Place is marked. This took its name from Lawrence Radford, who first built a house on the site about 1570. It ultimately gave its name to the whole district of Mount Radford.

Southernhay is shown as rather rough and uneven ground, with a pond or two in it, and was then called Croldiche. Coming around to the East

Gate, St Sidwell's is shown as built up well beyond the church and also running down Longbrook Street. This was almost entirely a working-class area from medieval times onwards.

Continuing around outside the walls, Northernhay also appears as very rough ground, a precipitous hillside dropping down to the Long Brook. It was levelled and laid out as a pleasant walk, with seats for the elderly, in the year 1612, so that it has been one of the attractive features of Exeter for well over a dozen generations.

Outside the North Gate a few houses straggled down a steep hill and up the other side towards St David's church, which stood in open country. Exe Street is shown as a lane running along the banks of the Long Brook down to the river, and above it was Mount Dinham, then called Weare Cliffs.

Inside the city the map shows the streets and houses only in a rather conventional way, and the details cannot be taken too literally. There are, however, some very interesting things on it. Coombe Street is shown, for example, with an open stream running down the middle of it and through an opening in the city wall to discharge into the leat below. This is the ancient stream which formerly rose in a spring right underneath the cathedral walls. But by 1587 the upper part of the stream had been lost, and it seems to be coming out of the ground at the top of Coombe Street. In 1611 the city Chamber ordered a pump to be made in Coombe Street (which was often called by the alternative name of Rock Lane), and this may be the date when the open stream was finally covered over.

There was still a good deal of open ground in this part of the city on which cloths were laid out on racks for drying (hence Rack Street). It had not yet become the congested slum area which it was destined to be by the early 19th century. Coming up South Street, an imposing building of considerable size is shown just where the Roman Catholic church now

43 Larkbeare, 'The Elizabethan House'.

stands. This was the town house of the Abbots of Tavistock, later known as the *Bear Inn*. Usually the abbots let it to substantial Exeter merchants, such as Edward Bridgeman, who took a long lease in 1535. After the dissolution of the monasteries and the confiscation of their lands, the *Bear Inn* eventually came into lay ownership. It had ceased to be an inn before 1825.

Continuing up South Street, St George's Church is shown, and from there to the top of South Street the street was called Cook Row. Here in medieval times the cooks of the city must have congregated. Milk Street is shown, but there is no Market Street. Where Market Street now runs, and where the Lower Market was built in the 1830s, was the Shambles, where the town and country butchers did their slaughtering and sold their meat.

On one side of the Shambles, fronting Smythen Street, was Butcher Row. Nothing of this survives today though some older citizens may possibly just be able to recall it. This was a row of 19 butchers' shops built by the city fathers as a piece of municipal enterprise in the year 1499 or 1500. In the High Street the Guildhall still awaited its porticoed Elizabethan front, as we see it today. This was built in 1593-6 at a total cost of £789.

When one looks at this map in detail, all sorts of interesting buildings are to be seen, but with few exceptions they are not named, and we can only speculate as to what they once were. It is a great pity that we have no description of the city, street by street, to go with this map. Even so, enough material survives to write a whole book about Elizabethan Exeter, who lived in it, and what it looked like.

44 John Gendall's picture of Butcher Row being fumigated during the cholera epidemic.

CHAPTER SIX

Civil War and Commonwealth

The Line-up in Devon

THE CIVIL WAR is one of the great landmarks of English history and
it affected Devon more than most counties. The long struggle between
Charles I and his Parliament and the increasing bitterness between them
culminated in the winter of 1641-2. War was then inevitable and the city
of Exeter, already suffering from a depression in the cloth trade, viewed
the prospect with regret and alarm. Charles left London to collect troops
in the North and on 22 August 1642 he declared war at Nottingham. Far
away, at Exeter, the city fathers began to organise their defences since they
were responsible for the key city of the South-West, the gateway to the
whole peninsula.

In the South-West of England, and in Devon particularly, feelings were
sharply divided between the King and Parliament. Generally speaking, the
peerage and the greater gentry were for the King, and the lesser gentry
and townspeople were for Parliament. But it was not even as simple as
this because we find on the parliamentarian side the Earl of Bedford, the
Rolles (the largest landowners in Devon), the Bampfyldes, the Drakes, and
others; and on the royalist side a considerable part of the population of
Exeter were to be found, as well as some of the most eminent gentry in
Devon, such as the Aclands. the Fulfords, the Poles, and the Seymours.
Sometimes even families were divided. The Fortescues in North Devon
were all parliamentarian, but those in South Devon were all royalist.

There must also have been a considerable number of the gentry and
others who were plain neutrals, unable to support either side wholeheartedly
or simply waiting to see which way the wind was going to blow. The
final line-up when the war started was therefore rather complicated in
Devon; but one could say that the important town of Plymouth was
strongly parliamentarian and so was Barnstaple, the leading town in North
Devon. At Exeter, too, there was a strong Puritan element which favoured
the parliamentarian cause, but the leading citizens were divided in their
sympathies. Many of the leading merchants were royalist, and the Dean and
Chapter were of course wholly royalist. With divided feelings on this scale,
it is not surprising that Devon was fought over for a long time during the
four years that the war lasted. At Exeter a special watch was maintained
day and night by 32 chosen citizens, supplies of corn and ammunition were

laid in, and the city walls were surveyed and repaired where necessary. The six guns of the city were mounted—not a very adequate defence for a mile and a half of walls.

By the end of 1642 Sir Ralph Hopton, the royalist commander, had cleared most of the South-West of parliamentary forces—all except Plymouth, Barnstaple, and Exeter. The failure to take Plymouth was probably decisive at this stage, because the plan for Hopton to advance on London from the west was impossible as long as that great port lay untaken in his rear. He had attacked Plymouth at the end of 1642 but had been defeated at Laira, just outside the town, and again at Modbury. At the very end of the year, he marched up to Exeter and called upon it to surrender. The mayor refused. The city was well prepared for a siege, Hopton was short of supplies, and he marched away without further ado.

The Siege of 1643

The rest of the first winter of the war passed quietly. Plymouth was undeniably for Parliament, but in the city of Exeter—just as in the Catholic rebellion of 1549—there remained a deep cleavage of sympathies. During the winter, however, the parliamentarians in the city gradually purged the chief offices of royalists, appointed a governor for the city, and began to make preparations for defending Exeter when the royalists should resume the attack.

The surrender of the rich city of Bristol to the King shook many of the parliamentarians. In Devon the Earl of Bedford tried to change sides and placed himself at the disposal of the King. Then a royalist victory at Stratton, just over the border in Cornwall, opened up the whole of Devon to their advance.

At Exeter, the Mayor, the Sheriff, and five aldermen, all of the parliamentary party, had been appointed commissioners for the city. As early as January they drew up elaborate instructions for its defence. The ammunition was to be checked and brought up to a satisfactory level, more gunners were to be procured, and also more companies of volunteers from the countryside around. Hand-picked men were to garrison and defend the castle. The ditches outside the city walls were made deeper and steeper. Ditches and drawbridges were made at each of the gates in order to prevent the enemy from blowing up the gates, and houses near the walls were destroyed in order to give a clear field of fire.

There were many instructions to reduce the danger of fire from enemy attack. All hay and straw was to be removed from around the Guildhall, and fire-fighting arrangements were brought up-to-date. Every household was told to take in as much fuel, corn, peas, and other foodstuffs as it could, and handmills were brought in from the country so that corn could be ground within the city while the siege was on. No women or children, or household goods, were to be allowed out of the city. A special force was kept in the Cathedral Yard with two sentinels on the top of the tower of St Mary Major. From here they could command a view of what was happening all around the city.

Steps were also taken to strengthen the defences of the city well outside it. Topsham and the river Exe were to be secured, and Powderham Castle, on the river, was either to be demolished or made safe for Parliament. Nearer to Exeter, Radford House, later to be called Mount Radford, was fortified. All the suburbs of the city were barricaded and fortifications were thrown up at Cowley Bridge and on St David's Hill All these and many other preparations show how determined the parliamentarians were to defend the capital of the West. Among other arrangements they ordered 'No bells to ring for any dead, or clocks to strike, while the city is besieged'.

The siege began on 19 June, when Sir John Berkeley closely surrounded the walled city. He was joined by Prince Maurice in late August and after a siege lasting 11 weeks in all the city surrendered on 4 September. The total cost to the city, as recorded in the siege accounts in the archives, was £18,479 12s. ½d. Part of this heavy bill was met by gifts from sympathisers, part from requisitions from the adherents of the other side, but most was borrowed at six per cent under the city's guarantee.

Sir John Berkeley became governor of the city, royalists who had been ousted from their offices (like the recorder) were restored, and the city had to support a royalist garrison at a cost of £40 a week, levied by a rate on the inhabitants.

45 The Tudor House.

Exeter, by reason of its importance and geographical position, became the royalist headquarters in the West, and a mint was set up in the city to coin money for the royalist forces. Silver and gilt plate was collected by local goldsmiths and others and converted into coin. For more than two and a half years the city remained virtually under military government, with an increasing friction and weariness as the months dragged by.

The year 1644 opened with the royalists in control of Exeter, with Plymouth still held by parliament, and with Barnstaple held by the royalists. Most of the county was in royalist hands and the main fighting of the civil war had moved elsewhere for a time. At Barnstaple the townspeople overpowered the royalist garrison in July and for a time the town passed into parliamentarian hands. Meanwhile the Queen had left Oxford which was threatened by parliamentarian forces, and had reached Exeter on 1 May 1644. Bedford House, the town house of the earls of Bedford in Exeter (occupying the site of the Dominican Friary which the Russells had acquired at the Dissolution), was placed at the disposal of the Queen who was expecting a child. This child was born at Bedford House and christened Henrietta in the cathedral on 21 July 1644. A new font was especially made for this royal occasion.

Prince Maurice was still held up outside Plymouth. In the summer the parliamentarians, under Lord Essex, again advanced towards the West. For some reason Essex did not attempt to take Exeter. He entered Devon at Axminster, marched on to Honiton and Cullompton and thence to Tiverton. From Tiverton he marched across hilly country to Crediton and on to Okehampton and Tavistock and so into Cornwall. King Charles was in pursuit and reached Exeter on 26 July. There he saw his infant daughter for the first time. The next day he went on to Crediton where he reviewed Prince Maurice's troops, and on 29 July resumed his march. He slept that night in an alehouse at Bow. This house (now a shop) still stands in the main street.

Charles caught up with Essex in Cornwall and defeated him at Lostwithiel. He returned to Exeter on 17 September, but departed for Oxford after a stay of a week. So ended the year 1644, with no important change in the balance of power in Devon, except that the royalists recaptured Barnstaple in September. It had been in parliamentary hands for only two months and now it remained a royalist garrison until the end of the war, when Fairfax re-took it in April 1646.

The war dragged on. Plymouth was still under siege. Trade was dislocated everywhere and country people were continually pillaged and plundered by the unpaid soldiers. Country houses suffered especially. Most people in Devon wanted the war to move on somewhere else or to come to an end. Up in the Midlands on 14 June 1645 there came a decisive defeat of the royalists at Naseby. The formidable new Model Army of Parliament was now free to deal with the tangled military situation in the South-West.

The Siege of 1645-6

One after another the great royalist strongholds fell, above all the city of Bristol in September. On 9 October Fairfax and his army had reached Chard, almost on the borders of Devon. Here they waited for two days for the wagons of money to catch them up. The troops had not been paid for some weeks and it was necessary to restore them to good humour. They were paid on Saturday night (11 October) and Chard must have been a wild place that night. On 13 October the army advanced to Axminster. There they learnt that the royalist commander, Lord Goring, intended to break out from Devon in order to join the King far to the east. Fairfax ordered a strict watch to be kept on all the roads from Exeter eastwards, but Lord Goring, Lord Wentworth, Lord Miller, and most of the bravest royalist cavalry, passed through Honiton about midnight and, by taking to the lanes across the Blackdown Hills, helped by the extreme darkness of the night, they got through.

Day by day Fairfax and his army moved forward into Devon—to Cullompton and then to Tiverton. Tiverton Castle fell without much of a struggle on 19 October, and on the next day Fairfax and the whole army marched seven miles south to the large village of Silverton. Here a council of war was held to decide whether to take the city of Exeter or go to the relief of Plymouth which had now been under siege for more than two years. Winter was coming on. The men were tired out with the continual marches and the sickness rate was rising. It was decided not to march so far west as Plymouth but to capture Exeter, especially as there were within the walls a thousand cavalry and eight thousand foot soldiers—too large a force to leave in the rear.

The decision having been taken by Fairfax to besiege Exeter, he went in person with a small party from Silverton to Stoke Canon. Thence he climbed Stoke Hill, up the old Tiverton road, until on the last summit of the hill he saw the fair city below him about a mile away. Here he meditated how best to make the attack, and thence he returned that night to his headquarters at Silverton.

Two days later (22 October) Fairfax, with a great part of his army, marched across country from Silverton to Newton St Cyres. He intended to go on to Alphington by the roads that skirted the city to the west, but the lanes were narrow, the days were growing short, and it was, as usual, raining. On the Thursday, the army marched up to a hilltop called the Beacon, probably the summit known as Waddlesdown on the Whitestone hills, still intending to get to Alphington, but the Devonshire rain in the unmade lanes bogged down the wagons. The army returned to Crediton with weary men, tired horses, and broken wagons. The Devonshire lanes and continual rain were giving Fairfax doubts about his plan to surround and attack Exeter. Another council of war was held at Crediton to discuss whether the plan should be followed through. While the discussion was going on around the table the door opened and 'Lieutenant-General Cromwell happily came in'. His forces were now on their way. He had come ahead of them while they were resting at Honiton.

It was agreed to go on with the plan to attack Exeter and for the next few days the troops were being disposed around the countryside. On Monday, 27 October, Fairfax and the army marched down to Topsham, passing well to the east of the city. Hearing this, the royalists burnt about eighty houses on the south side of Exeter to clear the ground outside the South Gate and to have a clear field of view. A number of gabled houses of late 17th-century date in Magdalen Street and Holloway Street survived until 1977. These houses were those that were built again after the war was over to replace those that had been destroyed. The *Valiant Soldier Inn** was one of these, and its name commemorates the ordinary soldiers of the Civil War.

It was decided to blockade Exeter all along the eastern side and not attempt to cross the Exe at this stage. Fairfax made his headquarters at Ottery St Mary and garrisons were set up at Nutwell, on the estuary of the Exe facing across to Powderham, and at Broadclyst, Poltimore, and Stoke Canon. In this way no help, either in food or men, could reach Exeter from the eastern side. It was then decided to move the main army to the west side of the city and the river, and to establish a chain of garrisons on that side which would complete the circle.

The first place chosen for attack on this side was Powderham. With both Nutwell and Powderham in their hands, the parliamentarians could prevent help reaching Exeter up the river. Under cover of darkness—it was nine o'clock on Sunday night, 14 December—Captain Dean with two hundred foot and dragoons moved across the river from Nutwell in boats and reached the Powderham side. But they found the Castle more strongly defended than they had imagined and they did not, in fact, attack it.

Not wishing to return without doing anything, they occupied the church, not far from the Castle. The next morning they brought provisions across the river from Nutwell into the church and began to fortify it. The royalists up at Exeter feared that the river would be blocked by these manoeuvres. On Monday night they sent down a party of five hundred soldiers to join the two hundred in the Castle. Together they attacked Fairfax's men who were barricaded inside the church, throwing in many hand grenades. For three hours the siege of Powderham church went on until the royalists withdrew, leaving the snow stained with their blood. However, it was bitterly cold in the church. There was no means of warming it, and the parliamentary forces were glad to be withdrawn in a day or two from this unpleasant situation.

Two other country houses on this side of Exeter were, however, taken over by the parliamentarians. One was Canonteign in the Teign Valley, and the other was Sir George Chudleigh's house at Ashton. So ended the year 1645.

* The *Valiant Soldier Inn* stood at the corner of Magdalen Street and Holloway Street. It was rebuilt after the Civil War was over and is referred to in 1651 in the Sessions Papers of the city. It was closed in March 1962 as it lay in the way of a road-widening scheme, and was demolished later in the same year. An inn stood on this corner for many centuries. The ground belonged to the Vicars Choral. In a lease of 1623 it was called the *Golden Lion*; another lease reveals that before that it was known as the *Goat*. It is not unusual for inns to change their names over many centuries. Robert Dymond wrote a valuable paper in 1880 on 'The Old Inns and Taverns of Exeter', but much more can now be said on this subject and it badly needs doing again, especially in view of the rapid changes and losses of recent years.

46 The junction of Magdalen Street and South Street *c.*1960. Nos. 36-39 Magdalen Street have since been demolished but Holy Trinity is used as a united services club.

47 The 17th-century *Valiant Soldier Inn* was demolished for road-widening.

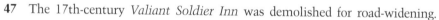

The siege of Exeter was interrupted once again by news that the royalists were advancing through the South Hams. Fairfax left sufficient forces to blockade the city, while the main army marched off to meet the royalists who had made their headquarters at Bovey Tracey. Cromwell himself went with them. The royalists were taken completely by surprise. It was almost supper-time when Cromwell and his men reached Bovey and the royalist officers were playing cards, so innocent were they of the whereabouts of the enemy. However, they got away. They threw their stake-money out of the window and whilst the Roundheads were scrambling for it, the officers escaped by a back door, across the river and into the night.

It was necessary to pursue the royalists and, above all, to capture Dartmouth which was in their hands. On the night of Sunday, 18 January, at eleven o'clock, the storming of Dartmouth began and was soon successful. Many prisoners were taken including Sir Hugh Pollard, the governor of the town, and the Earl of Newport and a great number of officers. Between eight hundred and a thousand ordinary soldiers were also captured but were released and told to go home. Large numbers of prisoners were only an embarrassment and these men were not likely to fight again. It was safe to let them go.

The army returned to the siege of Exeter. Almost immediately Powderham Castle surrendered to them. Once again the attack on Exeter was postponed by news that royalist cavalry were approaching from the Dorset side, and also that Lord Goring's forces were near Barnstaple in North Devon. There was a danger that these forces would join up. It was almost decided to storm the walls of Exeter and to finish the city off quickly. Things had gone so far that warrants were issued all around the countryside, commandeering all the ladders that could be found and also sending to Plymouth for their scaling ladders. Then further news came that the royalists were marching in full force to Torrington. It was necessary to do something about this quickly. Accordingly it was decided on 9 February, at another council of war, to blockade Exeter even more closely and to take the main part of the army off to North Devon to settle the royalists there. Strong garrisons were therefore left at Alphington and Peamore, and above all at Barley House, on the hill immediately overlooking the city from the west. Nothing could move around Exeter without being seen, nor could any help come up the river with the parliamentarians holding both Powderham and Nutwell, and also the fort at Exmouth.

The campaign in North Devon was very swift. Hopton was decisively defeated by Fairfax at Torrington on Monday, 16 February. Here the parish church was blown up. Hopton had stored in it nearly eighty barrels of gun powder and this was fired by 'a desperate villain, one Watts', who was paid £30 for the deed. The explosion blew up a good deal of the church. Fragments of masonry fell all over the town and in the fields. Most of the people who perished were prisoners in the church at the time, and the men who were guarding them.

Fairfax had to sleep the night at Stevenstone, the country house of the Rolles, as all the windows in Torrington had been blown out, and, we need hardly say, it was still raining. From here he moved rapidly into Cornwall

48 Poltimore House, photographed on 31 May 1960 when it was being used as a maternity hospital.

and cleared out the royalists there but it was not until Sunday, 29 March that he was able to return to Crediton to resume the siege of Exeter. That night part of the army moved on to Newton St Cyres, and a small party pushed on to occupy Heavitree, then a village well outside Exeter, in case the royalists should sally out from the city and burn it.

By Tuesday, Fairfax had drawn his whole army around the city within musket shot. He reviewed his men, going from post to post, amid great cheering and volleys of shot. He returned that night to his headquarters at Culm John—the house is now completely gone but the gateway is still there, near Killerton—and from there he wrote a letter to Sir John Berkeley calling upon him to surrender the city without any further bloodshed.

Sir John saw that it was hopeless to continue the struggle and he replied that he was willing to consider an honourable surrender. The parties met at Poltimore, the house of Sir John Bampfylde—we can still see this house, though sadly vandalised and awaiting restoration—and the articles of surrender were there drawn up.

It was agreed that the city should surrender to Sir Thomas Fairfax, that there should be no plundering of any citizen or countryman by the soldiers, and that the Princess Henrietta and her governess and household should be allowed to pass unmolested, with all their plate, money, and goods, to any place they wished. It was also agreed that neither the cathedral nor any of the parish churches of the city should be damaged or plundered in any way.

As for the royalist garrison, it was agreed 'that the governor, together with all lords, clergymen, gentlemen, captains, officers, troopers, and common soldiers, shall march out of the city on Monday next, the 13th of April, by twelve of the clock at noon, with their horses, full arms, bag and baggage, and their goods, colours flying, drums beating, matches lighted, bullets, full bandoliers, with sufficient convoys unto Oxford, or unto Helston in Cornwall ...'. Ordinary soldiers who did not wish to march out were allowed to give up their arms, except their swords, and to go home with bag and baggage, and were not to be compelled to take up arms against the king. War was a much more honourable and humane thing in those days.

Those citizens who had supported the royalist cause, or the more prominent among them, were heavily fined for their delinquency (as it was called). Thus Robert Walker, one of the richest merchants in the city, whose income had been reckoned at £500 a year, was eventually fined nearly £900—probably not far short of £500,000 today. Roger Mallock, the richest merchant in Exeter at this time, was fined over £1,600. The papers relating to these proceedings give us some idea of Exeter merchants' incomes in the 1640s. Mallock probably enjoyed nearly a thousand a year. John Colleton was reckoned to be worth £200 a year, James Rodd £300, George Potter £250. Several were assessed at £100 a year—probably this was about the average income for the merchant class (worth between £50,000 and £75,000)—and some small merchants were put down at £60 a year. Between the smallest merchants and the largest there was a very considerable range of income, just as there is today in the business class. One must not think of the 17th-century merchant class as too uniform a group of individuals. The richer were worth five to ten times the lesser.

Nearly three years later, on 30 January 1649, King Charles I was executed. England became a republic for the next 11 years, governed, until his death in September 1658, by Oliver Cromwell. Cromwell was undoubtedly a great and honourable man who did what he thought best for England, and who was rarely, if ever, guilty of the damage that is attributed to him, especially in our churches. Such damage as was done was inflicted by the worst type of Puritans who seem to have been especially strong in Devon. We can read about some of their activities in the county records, and their misguided attempts to make life uncomfortable for everybody. Years before, William Shakespeare, that great English humanist, had already weighed them up: 'Dost thou think, because thou art virtuous, there shall be no more cakes and ale?'

The war was over but Exeter was occupied by the military for another 14 years until the restoration of the monarchy in 1660. It was far too important to leave unguarded. There was always a risk of a royalist rising. Indeed, all through the Commonwealth period the western royalists hoped to recapture Exeter, but there was never any serious danger of its happening. The citizens were heartily sick of war, which apart from all else had utterly crippled their trade in all directions. Slowly the damage was repaired, and old connections picked up again, but on the whole the Protectorate was a time of depression and there was still a heavy debt—over £14,000—hanging over from the days of the great siege in 1643. But there was one bright spot: Exeter had got a good foothold in the Netherlands markets, and the new manufacture of perpetuana-serges was destined to sweep all before it.

Printing in Exeter

It was not all a gloomy tale, those Civil War years. Among the odd sidelights of the war we had the worthy Dr Thomas Fuller here for a couple of years. He came to Exeter after the capture of the city by the royalists in September 1643. The king appointed him chaplain to the household of the infant Princess Henrietta Maria who was still living at Bedford House. Dr Fuller, cheerful and corpulent, with bright blue eyes and flaxen hair, preached in various of our churches and wrote his books. Here he probably went on preparing his *Worthies of England*, the book by which he is best known, and here he completed *Good Thoughts in Bad Times*. This book, less well known, is notable as the first ever to be printed in Exeter. It was printed for Thomas Hunt, bookseller in St Peter's churchyard (the Close), in the year 1645.

Actually it was printed on a travelling press which was set up in Exeter in the royalist cause. So far as we know at present the first resident printer does not appear in the city until 1683 and we do not know his name. A printer with the initials 'J.B.' printed the speech of William of Orange to the gentry who joined him in 1688. He is thought to be one John Baker. The first resident printer whose name is known for certain is Samuel Darker who printed a book in the year 1698. Since 1683 the city has never lacked a resident printer and printing is today a substantial industry.

It should be said, for the sake of completeness, that the first printing-press of which we have any record in Exeter is that of the rector of St Edmund's. He was John Williams and he had probably been a monk at Tavistock Abbey until its dissolution in 1539. We then lose sight of him, but in 1554 he was appointed to the living of St Edmund's at Exeter and here he stayed until his death in 1572. In his will he bequeathed his printing equipment and tools to his cousin. Very probably he had brought these from the abbey, which had set up the first printing press in Devon, so we may assume that there was a press in Exeter in 1554. Whether he ever used it here is another matter: no book has ever been discovered with an Exeter imprint at this early date.

CHAPTER SEVEN

A Georgian City

Two Visitors to Exeter

THE CIVIL WAR and its aftermath did great damage to the trade of Exeter, but by 1660 the city was recovering and indeed was entering upon its most prosperous age. It was still one of the largest provincial towns in England. Norwich and York were the largest, then came Bristol and Newcastle, and fifth in size came the city of Exeter. Its mainstay was still the cloth trade but its principal market had shifted from France to Holland.

Celia Fiennes came to Exeter in the year 1698 and gives us a description of the busy and important city as she saw it.

> Exeter is a town very well built. The streets are well pitched, spacious noble streets, and a vast trade is carried on … there is an incredible quantity of serges made and sold in the town. Their market day is Friday which supplies with all things like a fair almost. The market for meat, fowl, fish, garden things, and dairy produce takes up three whole streets, besides the large market house set on stone pillars which runs a great length, on which they lay their packs of serges. Just by it is another walk within pillars which is for the yarn. The whole town and country is employed for at least twenty miles around in spinning, weaving, dressing and scouring, fulling and drying of the serges. It turns the most money in a week of anything in England. One week with another, there is £10,000 paid in ready money, sometimes £15,000 …

She goes on to give a description of the woollen industry in its various processes at Exeter, which was chiefly concerned with the dyeing and finishing and not with the actual manufacture. She thought the city was very much like London, and speaks particularly of 'an exchange full of shops like our exchanges are'. And there was also a very large space railed in near the cathedral with walks around it which was called the Exchange for Merchants. Here the Exeter merchants met regularly twice a day to discuss business just as the merchants of London did.

At the time of Celia Fiennes' visit, the city fathers were engaged in making big improvements to the canal and the quay. The original canal had always been rather unsatisfactory and many merchants preferred to unload their goods at Topsham and to bring them up by road. The first step was to extend the canal from Countess Wear and to deepen it. Then the quay was extended to its present length and a Custom House was built in

49 The Custom House.

1681 to complete the scene. This Custom House, one of the handsomest buildings in Exeter, was the first building to be completed in brick and is notable in this respect also. It originally had a colonnaded front, behind which goods could be placed in wet weather. At a later date the openings between the pillars were filled in with brick as we see them today. Celia Fiennes goes on: 'you ascend up a handsome pair of stairs into a large room full of desks and little partitions for the writers and accountants. It is full of books and files of paper.' This is the Long Room which has perhaps the finest remaining plaster ceiling in Exeter, a splendid baroque affair by the Devon plasterer John Abbot.

About a dozen or so years after Celia Fiennes' visit, the celebrated Daniel Defoe came to Exeter in the course of his travels round England and Wales. The first thing he noticed about the city was that it united two things seldom found in the same town --- 'Tis full of gentry and good company, and yet full of trade and manufactures also. The serge market held here every week is very well worth a stranger seeing, and next to the Brigg market at Leeds in Yorkshire, is the greatest in England. The people assured me that at this market is generally sold from 60 to 70 to 80, and sometimes a hundred thousand pounds value in serges in a week.' These figures are pretty certainly exaggerated but the Devonshire woollen industry was still the most important branch of the woollen manufacture of England.

Defoe notes that by the time of his visit, which was probably about 1714, the canal had been widened and deepened and extended to Topsham, and that ships could now come right up to the city and load and unload there. Besides the Dutch market, Exeter had a great trade with Portugal, Spain and Italy. From Portugal and Spain came back wine which laid the foundation of more than one fortune among Exeter merchants.

'Exeter is a large, rich, beautiful, populous, and was once a very strong city.' But Defoe notes that the castle, the walls, and all the old fortifications were now demolished—this, of course, was not true, but they were probably in great disrepair because the days of walled towns were now over. Warfare was now so different that Exeter at its strongest could not now hold out five days against a siege. 'Nay,' says Defoe, 'it would hardly put an army to the trouble of opening trenches against it at all.'

Between the visit of Celia Fiennes and that of Defoe, Exeter got its first newspapers. Norwich was the first provincial city to establish a newspaper (1701), with Bristol close behind (1702). The oldest surviving copy of an Exeter newspaper is No. 556 of Sam Farley's *Exeter Post-Man*, dated 10 August 1711 and printed 'at my House near the New-Inn'. There is good evidence for saying that Farley had started this newspaper in the year 1704. An American newspaper, the *Boston News-Letter*, was started in April of that year, and 12 months later the editor, in reviewing his paper's progress, compared it with a newspaper at Exeter 'where they began to print much about the same time that we began here'. So Exeter can boast of the third newspaper to be started in the provinces.

Another early newspaper was Jos. Bliss's *Exeter Post-Boy*, which first appeared in 1707; and there is a surviving copy of the *Exeter Mercury*, printed by Philip Bishop 'at his Printing-Office in St Peter's Church-Yard' in 1714. Poor Bishop died two years later in the King's Bench Prison in London, having been arrested for printing a Jacobite ballad. At this time, when there were hardly a score of newspapers outside London, Exeter had no fewer than three.

Three Exeter newspaper editors were summoned before the House of Commons in December 1718 for breach of privilege in printing items from the proceedings of the House. They were George Bishop, Joseph Bliss, and Andrew Brice, who humbly acknowledged their offences and were discharged.

Andrew Brice is a notable Exeter figure. He had been apprenticed to Bliss, but had run away and in 1717, when he was not yet 25 years of age, he founded his own paper *The Post-Master: or The Loyal Mercury*. This was the paper that got him into trouble. In 1725 he began publishing the newspaper by which perhaps he is chiefly known, *Brice's Weekly Journal*. These early newspapers were small and contained little or no local news, but the advertisements in *Brice's Weekly Journal* are of considerable local interest, especially the descriptions of houses and other property for sale or to be let.

Exeter Merchant Families

Exeter's commercial prosperity was at its height in the first quarter of the 18th century. Enterprising and able young men came to the city from all parts as they had done in Tudor times, and there was, too, a steady influx of young men from Germany, Holland, and Switzerland who eventually became merchants in Exeter and contributed much to the life of the city. Among the young Devonians to come into Exeter in these years of booming trade and high profits was the first William Kennaway, a name that could still be seen above the wine merchants' premises in Palace Gate until the late 1970s. Young Kennaway walked into the teeming city in the summer of 1713. He does not seem to have served a seven-year apprenticeship, for in August of that year he was admitted to the freedom of the city as a serge-maker on his own account. He married about eighteen months later.

His son William (1718-93) followed him as a serge-maker but branched out on a wider scale altogether and in 1743 founded the merchanting business which has been so long associated with their name. His account books survive. They are now in the city library and cover the period from 1751 to his death in 1793. His system of accounting is a rather home-made one but is tolerably easy to follow. At any rate, the steady growth of his business is clearly revealed year by year.

50 Kennaway's Wine and Spirit Merchants were at Palace Gate until 1975. Barrels were brought up from the Quay for the contents to be bottled here.

The business was still a very modest one in 1751: total assets (including his house and furniture, wool in the warehouse, and so forth) only amounted to a little under £2,400, and his liabilities to just over £1,000. The credit balance for that year was £1,382 4s. 6d. In the first ten years covered by the accounts (1751-60), the credit balance or total capital rose to £4,614 10s. 0d.—an annual increase of about £323. Over the next ten years the annual increase of assets amounted to £743 on an average, and there was little change in this rate of increase all through the 1770s. But the next decade saw a spectacular expansion of the business, the annual increase in the capital averaging about £1,825. In some good years the business made over £3,000.

William Kennaway senior took his two sons into the business as they came of age and ultimately a third son, all of whom were given a share in the profits and assets. In 1786 William Kennaway senior, now nearing the age of seventy, reckoned that the whole business was worth £31,600, of which his own share amounted to nearly £26,000. His eldest son's share was worth between £4,000 and £5,000. By the early 1790s there were four Kennaways in the business and they were worth about £43,000 between them. The greater part of their business was now with Italy and Spain: of the total assets (in 1792) of £83,000 odd, the Italian customers owed over £28,000 and the Spanish just over £10,000.

It had taken William Kennaway about forty years to build up a successful business in the 18th century. He had come to it just too late for the most prosperous days of the woollen trade, when progress might have been quicker, but he had started from next to nothing and his achievement was a very solid one. Like other Exeter merchants he used some of his later fortune to establish a private bank, in this case the Western Bank. His son William (1751-1819) carried on the family business of merchanting and banking, but in his day the Exeter woollen trade practically collapsed as a result of the Napoleonic wars. and the business turned almost entirely to the importing of wine and let the woollen trade go. It is a pity that the account-books for these critical years do not survive, for it would have been instructive to see how the business weathered the storm and reoriented itself. A younger son, John Kennaway (1758-1836), entered the employment of the East India Company and made his name and fortune like so many other able young Englishmen in that profitable field. He showed himself to be a successful diplomatist and was rewarded with a baronetcy in 1791; returning to England he founded a landed family at Escot, near Ottery St Mary, with an estate of some 4,000 acres. The Kennaways still flourish at Escot.

In the next generation the Exeter branch of the family mostly entered the professions. William Kennaway (1796-1868) carried on the family business of wine-merchanting until his death. He was the mayor of Exeter in the awful year of the cholera—1832—when he set a fine example of public service at a critical time. Mark Kennaway (1793-1875) became a solicitor with a very wide and lucrative practice especially among the landed families of the neighbourhood, and was the acknowledged leader of the Liberal party in Exeter for the greater part of his life. Other Kennaways became soldiers and parsons. All this, however, was a long way in the future when the first William Kennaway came into Exeter to seek his fortune in the palmy days of Queen Anne.

The Kennaways in their early days seem to have been nonconformist. Mark Kennaway was baptised in the Unitarian chapel—George's Meeting in South Street—in the spring of 1793, though in later life he became what is always called, for some inscrutable reason, 'staunch Church of England'. The early nonconformists, above all the Presbyterians, formed a very numerous and valuable element in Exeter commercial society. They were able men of independent thought and frugal habits, debarred from all municipal office and from the universities by reason of their religious views. With so much of English life closed to them, their great energies and abilities went into single-minded business activity, and here they generally flourished.

Among the foreigners who were attracted to Exeter in the early 18th century were some names that were afterwards to become well known. Most notable of all were John Baring, a Lutheran from Bremen in north Germany, and John Duntze, also from Bremen. John Baring arrived as a young man of 20 in 1717, four years after the young Kennaway, and was apprenticed to Edmund Cock, a serge-maker and a Presbyterian in the parish of Holy Trinity. Early in 1727 he married the only daughter and heiress of John Vowler, a rich grocer who was also a strong Presbyterian. John Vowler had built for himself the charming little house called Bellair on the Topsham Road, then in the open country. This perfect little Queen Anne house, built about 1710, is now engulfed in the new buildings of the Devon County Council (1957-64) but it is still worth seeking out.

It is not difficult to imagine where John Baring and Elizabeth Vowler first met, for it was almost certainly in the new Meeting House in James Street, which had been erected by the Presbyterians in 1687 as their principal place of worship. James Street has disappeared under Western Way. But it once had some good houses—older citizens will remember them well— and the Presbyterians who were on the whole a comfortably-off body, chose to build their principal meeting house here when the Declaration of Indulgence (1687) allowed them and all other nonconformists freedom of worship. Their new chapel was called James' Meeting, out of gratitude to King James II, and the whole street got its name as a consequence. This chapel was abandoned when the Presbyterians built their new chapel in South Street in 1760, calling it George's Meeting in honour of King George III. This is the best surviving

51 Bellair.

52 George's Meeting, soon to be a pub.

example in Devon of an 18th-century nonconformist chapel, retaining as it does many of its original internal fittings, including the beautiful pulpit which had been taken over from James's Meeting. George's Meeting closed in 1987 and was used as an antiques market. It is now to become a pub.

To return, however, to John Baring: with the backing of a rich father-in-law and his wife's intelligence and handsome dowry, he had got off to a good start, with the result that, at the time of his early death in 1748, he was the most eminent merchant in the city. At first he lived in Palace Gate and he and the first William Kennaway must have known each other well. Then in 1737 he was able to buy the mansion of Larkbeare, which stood at the foot of Holloway Street. This street still contains some very good 18th-century merchants' houses, sometimes tucked away in places where one has to look for them. In the same year, John Baring bought the advowson of the small parish of St Leonard's, and some land in that parish.

Larkbeare had belonged to another Exeter merchant, Andrew Lavington, who had gone bankrupt. Not every Exeter merchant made a fortune in those days; some indeed were badly caught out in the South Sea Bubble in which they lost a great deal of money. The Barings retained Larkbeare down to 1832 but they moved to Mount Radford in the second generation. John Baring the second (1729-1816) inherited a very good business from his father and expanded it greatly. He completed his education in Geneva, travelled extensively on the continent to enlarge his commercial knowledge, and returned to his native city in 1757 at the age of twenty-eight. He had also inherited the intelligence and commercial abilities of both his parents, for his mother had played a considerable part, not only with her money, in building up the Baring business in the first generation.

With his younger brother Francis (1749-1810), John Baring started a business in London as a wool importer in connection with his Larkbeare factory. The London end of the business developed under the genius of Francis Baring into a merchant-banking firm, which during the Napoleonic wars and immediately afterwards became world-famous under the name of Baring Brothers. (The bank was brought down in 1995 by a rogue trader.) The Barings went on to make millions as merchant bankers and to blossom out in the 20th century into no fewer than six distinct peerages.

The elder brother, John, retired from London to Exeter where, like other successful woollen manufacturers, he established a private bank—the Devonshire Bank. In the year 1770 he bought the manor of Heavitree, which included the whole of Mount Radford and much else, from Arthur Kelly esquire, whose family had held it for centuries. Almost the whole parish of St Leonard's became Baring property. During the 1770s he converted the original Elizabethan house, built by Lawrence Radford about 1570, into a handsome red-brick Georgian mansion. This stood until 1902 when it was demolished to make way for Barnardo Road, but the front lawn of the house still remains as an open green space in front of that road, the last relic of the days of the Barings in Exeter.

John Baring died in 1816. The Baring property in and around Exeter passed to Sir Thomas Baring, who had no particular associations with the city. When the great building boom of the 1820s came, Sir Thomas was able to sell his Exeter estate for a considerable sum of money to various builders who developed this part of the city. The name Baring is commemorated in various places in this part of Exeter. St Leonard's Road was originally the carriage drive of the Barings, leading in from Magdalen Road along a graceful curve down to their mansion.

53 Mount Radford House, built by John Baring *c*.1775. It became a school in 1827 (as shown here) and was demolished in 1902.

Church and Chapel

The number of nonconformists in early Georgian Exeter was considerable, probably over a quarter of the total population. The Presbyterians were the largest and most influential body amongst them, with no fewer than three meeting houses; but the oldest were probably the Baptists, who have an unbroken history in our city since 1656, and perhaps earlier than that. The Quakers (Society of Friends) were nearly as old in the South-West: in October 1656 no fewer than 20 of their number were in prison at Exeter, and they were well organised by the 1670s.

In the year 1744 the Bishop sent to all the clergy of his diocese a list of questions for them to answer. The replies from the Exeter clergy tell us a good deal about the strength of nonconformity in the city as well as about church services and schools of all kinds. Some of the Exeter clergy disliked the nonconformists very much and made it plain. The rector of St Mary Steps, for example, reported: 'I have, upon the best calculation I can make, in my parish about 200 families. And of them, I thank God, I have not more than four whole families of Dissenters of any kind.' The neighbouring parish of St Edmund was also poor and crowded and the rector similarly disdainful of Dissenters. This parish contained between three and four hundred families 'and of them, I thank God, I have not more than five or six families of Dissenters of every kind.' Most of the Exeter clergy, however, accepted and spoke of the nonconformists with respect, as indeed they well might. In some parishes the Dissenters were very strong: the rich parish of St Petrock, for example, had 55 families in all, of whom no fewer than 21 were Dissenters of one sort or another.

St Stephen's was a rich little parish in the centre of the city. The rector reported that it contained about 56 families at this date, of whom five were Presbyterians. There was no chapel or charity school in the parish, but he mentions that there was 'a boarding school for young Ladies', the only one of its kind in the city. The rector lived in the Precinct of Bradninch, then a secluded row of pleasant houses, in preference to the rectory house in his parish, of which he says, 'It is so mean and ordinary that I doubt if the minister did ever live in it.' The standard of churchmanship at St Stephen's was fairly high—in quantity at least. Divine Service was performed twice every Sunday, and prayers were said twice in the week on Wednesdays and Saturdays, as well as on Holy Days. Communion was administered regularly once a month as well as at the great feasts of Christmas, Easter, and Whitsun.

The number of communicants on the whole was surprisingly high. In the lower part of the city the two parishes of St Edmund and St Mary Steps had a monthly communion in turn, which was received by about a hundred people on each occasion and by about 120 to 140 at Easter.

One of the questions asked of the Exeter clergy concerned any charity school or public school within their parishes. From their replies we discover that there were altogether ten charity or public schools in addition to the private boarding school already mentioned. The rector of St Edmund's reported that there was no charity school in his parish but a 'Publick

School' in which 'the master, Mr James Rouse, teaches children to write and cypher, and I believe the number of them may be about twenty. I do not know or hear that he takes any care either as to the Principalls or Moralls of his children, and as to bringing them duly to church as the Canon directs, he never does and but seldom comes himself.'

In St Mary Arches parish there was a school for Poor Maidens, called Hele's Hospital, in which the number of children varied; and there was another charity school for girls in the same parish. In the neighbouring parish of St Olave, there was a charity school for forty girls and 'another charity school wherein thirty children of the city are taught to read the English Protestant Bible'. The large parish of St Mary Major with over 400 families did not contain a school of any kind.

In St Mary Steps parish there was one public school in which ten children were taught to read and spell out of a charity administered by the rector, and about twenty more at the expense of their own friends or relations. 'These children are carefully taught and instructed not only to read and spell well, but also to understand the principles of the Christian Religion as explained in our Church Catechism and are duly brought to church as the Canon requires. There is also another reading school in this parish supported by the charity of the Dissenters.' In St Paul's parish there was a charity school, consisting of 50 boys, which was maintained by subscription. This was one of the charity schools founded by Bishop Offspring Blackall in 1709, known afterwards as the Episcopal Schools. Bishop Blackall had founded four schools, two for boys and two for girls, which were afterwards reduced to one of each. Two hundred and fifty years after their foundation there were still two Episcopal Schools, in modern premises, on Mount Dinham. They were taken over by the Technical College when the school system was reorganised in the 1970s.

A few years before this episcopal enquiry, John Wesley had made his first visit to Exeter and virtually founded Methodism here. He had preached in one of the churches—either St Mary Major or St Mary Arches, and most probably the former—on Sunday morning, 24 November 1739. The rector debarred him from preaching at the afternoon service on the ground that his doctrines, though true, were dangerous and likely to lead to 'enthusiasm'. But the seed had been sown. The Old Nonconformity had little attraction for those not born into its ranks: the new gospel preached that salvation was by God's grace free to all. It offered something to the mass of ordinary people that the Anglican Church could not (or would not), and something less austere and intellectual than the Old Nonconformity. But the Methodists, as they later came to be called, had a hard struggle to survive in a bigoted city like Exeter. In May 1745, for example, they were beaten up for days on end by an ignorant mob. Neither the city clergy nor the magistrates made any effort to restrain the brutal, loutish element, who indeed had some support among the merchant class. The whole treatment of Wesley and the early Methodist worshippers makes sad reading in Exeter history. It shows us at our very worst, with the loutish element too often allowed to get out of hand. The Exeter Methodists remained weak in numbers until the end of the century. None of their

54 The Mint Wesleyan Chapel, opened in 1813.

early chapels or meeting-houses has survived. The rather grand Mint Chapel in Fore Street, built in 1812, was considerably altered in Victorian days. The new style of decoration from 1898 was characterised sadly by one old member as 'rather too suggestive of a music-hall'. The church was replaced by a modern building in 1969-70.

A Changing City

Georgian Exeter was still one of the leading cities of England, wealthy, lively, bustling, as narrow as its streets in some respects (where the ignorant mob was involved as in the Methodist riots) but in the forefront of many movements where there was a proper leadership. In the first days of the year 1741 a new Dean reached Exeter—Dr Alured Clarke, who had been a prebendary of Winchester where he had founded a noble public hospital five years earlier. Dr Clarke resolved 'not to give sleep to his eyes, nor slumber to his eyelids' until he had founded a hospital at Exeter, and he began campaigning at once. By 23 July the first general meeting of the subscribers was held in the chapter house of the cathedral, with the Dean in the chair, possible sites for the hospital were examined and the lower end of Southernhay chosen; and the foundation-stone was laid on 27 August. Rarely can a great enterprise have been carried through so swiftly and surely as this:

> The foundation stone was laid in a very solemn manner, a great number of Gentlemen, Benefactors to this Charity, assembled in the Chapter House, from whence they went in procession to Southernhay, where a party of soldiers were drawn up, who saluted them with

55 The Royal Devon and Exeter Hospital of 1741 in Southernhay, now Dean Clarke House.

three vollies of small arms. The stone was then laid by Dean Clarke, assisted by Humphrey Sydenham, Esq., Member for this city, and other gentlemen who acted as proxies for John Tuckfield, Esq., in the presence of several thousands of spectators. The ceremony being ended the Dean made an excellent and solemn oration on the occasion, offering up his prayers to the Almighty for success in the undertaking, recommending to those who were in affluent circumstances, the duty of assisting the poor in time of sickness, and exhorting the poor to be obedient to their superiors, and grateful to their benefactors. The Cathedral and other bells were rung on the occasion, general gladness prevailed amongst every class of people. Thus by the zealous endeavours of this excellent divine, the Devon and Exeter Hospital justly owes its foundation; an institution which will always reflect honour on its promoters.

The architect of the new hospital was an Exeter man, Mr John Richards. There were no architects as such in Exeter at this time. Builders like Hooper, Stribling, and Nosworthy, to name three men who stamped their character upon Georgian Exeter, were their own architects. They had a natural good taste as well as a long training. No builder today can begin to compare with them in this respect. John Richards, who had been born in the remote North Devon village of Mariansleigh, received 'some little instruction at a Grammar School, but his Genius chiefly inclining him to Mathematical Studies he was apprenticed with a joiner in St Thomas's (Exeter) who also made and sold Gunter's Scales and Sea--Quadrants.' This joiner was one Abraham Voysey, whose widow John Richards subsequently married at the age of twenty. By this means he succeeded to a good business as a joiner and builder 'for which he was the better qualified by his proficiency in Geometry and Architecture.' It was as a builder that he

56   The second Exe Bridge (1775-1905).

drew the designs for, and built, the Devon and Exeter Hospital, but he soon afterwards relinquished that trade and was from the 1740s onwards chiefly a surveyor and valuer. For several years towards the end of his life he was hopelessly insane and died so in January 1778 in his 88th year.

Once the building was begun, subscriptions flowed in and the work went on speedily. The committee met weekly in the upper room at Mol's Coffee House. On the first day of January 1743 the hospital opened its doors, to two out-patients—Mary Croote and John Elliott. Five days later four in-patients were admitted and the endless work of the hospital had begun. Dean Clarke never lived to see his noble foundation completed, for he died in the summer of 1742 at the early age of forty-six. His portrait is in the Board Room of the original hospital on Southernhay, now NHS offices bearing his name; but his true memorials are the great hospitals at Winchester and Exeter.

The pace of change in Exeter quickened remarkably in the latter half of the 18th century. One by one the ancient gates were demolished, beginning with the North Gate in 1769, but it was exactly 50 years before the last of them—the South or 'Great Gate'—went, in the year 1819.* It is a vast pity that this magnificent gateway, one of the most impressive things of its kind in England, should have been destroyed like this and not by-passed as it could easily have been. Through this gateway many kings of England had passed from William the Conqueror onwards: it ranked with the cathedral, the castle, and the guildhall, as one of the grandest monuments of the Middle Ages in Exeter.

New roads were being opened out, especially new entrances to the city. A new Exe Bridge, on a different line from the old, was opened in 1778, and the city walls were breached so as to make a direct approach to the bridge—New Bridge Street. Inside the city, crescents and terraces were being built apace. Best known of all was Bedford Circus, one of the most notable pieces of Georgian town-planning in England. This was begun in 1773 by Mr Robert Stribling, an Exeter builder. At first it was simply a crescent (on the north side) of 'fourteen genteel houses'. The original plan had been for a circus, but the southern side was not in fact built until 1824-6. Bedford Circus was severely damaged by the Germans in May 1942 but it could have been rescued and rebuilt had the good will been present: its final destruction was an unforgivable act of vandalism.

One of the many improvements in the city was the building of fine new Assembly Rooms by Mr William Mackworth Praed in the year 1769, now the *Royal Clarence Hotel*. This became the first hostelry in England to be called an hotel, the name being first used in an advertisement dated 7 September 1770. There Peter Berlon, the French proprietor, returns thanks to the nobility and gentry for favours received. 'The very great success he

* The East Gate went in 1784, the West Gate and Water Gate in 1815.

has met with since he converted his House into an INN, gives him Hopes
that ... the Undertaking will not fail having the desired Effect.' For a long
time his establishment was known simply as *The Hotel*, even the *New
London*—its great rival—describing itself as an inn.

Next door to the new hotel, on the corner of Martin's Lane, was the
Exeter Bank, the earliest of several banks to be established in the city.
This opened its doors on 9 July 1769, its partners being Sir John Duntze
(who had made a fortune in the woollen trade), William Mackworth Praed,
Joseph Sanders, and Daniel Hamilton. The original building still stands,
incorporated into the *Royal Clarence Hotel*. In the following year John
Baring and others established the Devonshire Bank. Next in date (1786)
was the City Bank established by the Milfords and Nations, both Unitarian
families. The General Bank (1792) was founded by Mr Joshua Williams,
'a serge merchant of great respectability', together with the Sparkes, who
were relatives. All the partners were members of the Society of Friends.
Joshua Williams junior had lately returned from India with a fortune, which
doubtless helped to establish the new bank firmly. And finally, a fifth bank
was founded by the Kennaways. This opened its doors on 1 January 1793
as The Western Bank. What is notable about these early Exeter banks is
that they were all founded by men who had made a modest fortune in the
woollen trade, helped out in at least two cases (Kennaways and Williams)
by fortunes made in India, and very largely if not entirely by men who
were nonconformists of one kind or another. These were the men who
were debarred from much of public life and many of the professions by
the bigotry of the law and the ancient universities.

'The spirit of improvement', which had demolished the ancient gates of
the city and erected many handsome new buildings, expressed itself in a
multitude of ways. The roads leading from the city were slowly improved,
the earliest act of several for this purpose being passed in 1753. In 1760
an act was obtained 'for enlightening the streets of Exeter' with oil-lamps.
By 1768 there were 168 lamps in the city, far too few and too feeble but
far better than the total darkness (except at full moon) of earlier centuries.
Pavements were made in the chief streets for the first time in 1778. But
the streets remained filthy and unsavoury, especially in dry weather, and
not until 1807 was the first sewer laid, in the High Street.

Meanwhile the speed of transport increased steadily. In 1658 the journey
to London took four days. A hundred years later it took two days, at a
single fare of 45s. Then, in the autumn of 1785, came the first mail-coaches,
which made the run from Exeter to London in 24 hours, carrying no outside
passengers. The old coaches had averaged four miles an hour; these did nine
miles an hour and there were many old-fashioned critics of this mania for
speed. One letter to the local newspaper expressed astonishment 'that any
rational person will venture a life in any of those destructive and dangerous
vehicles ... Could no line be drawn between melancholy and madness?
No balance struck from moving to flying? What! must we jump from four
miles to nine within the hour?'

Not all could afford the dangerous speed of the mail-coach (and it could
be dangerous: upsets were frequent). For these there were (in 1800) coaches

like the *Mercury* which left the *New London Inn* at 3.45 every morning and reached London the next day at noon (32½ hours in all). The single fare was 70s. outside, 38s. inside, with luggage charged at 2½d. a pound. On the *London Mail* the fares were four guineas and 43s. respectively, with luggage at 3d. a pound. There were, of course, slower coaches also, at correspondingly reduced fares.

Local journeys were leisurely affairs. The diligence from Exeter to Barnstaple via South Molton took eight hours in 1778. To go from Exeter to Bristol took one and a half days in 1768, reduced to one day in 1777 at a single fare of 21s. For long-distance goods traffic, Thomas Russell's Fly Wagons—the equivalent of our lorries—took four days for the London journey in the 1780s. Russell had a tremendous establishment in South Street, the biggest of its kind in the South-West.

Other minor changes may be noted: street-names were put up for the first time in 1804, and houses numbered in the principal streets. But the Exeter directory for 1828 shows that even a quarter of a century later only the principal streets had numbered houses, together with a rather haphazard selection of lesser streets and terraces. Gas-lighting first appeared in the streets and principal shops in the summer of 1817. In 1794 the city saw the building of the largest and most commodious inn it had yet seen—the *New London Inn*, built for Mr John Land, the proprietor, by Matthew Nosworthy. This immediately became not only the most important inn in the city but a centre of social and political life throughout the 19th century. When Mr Land died on 24 January 1817 at the age of 87, he was the oldest and wealthiest innkeeper in the West of England, and his funeral (at Pinhoe) was an astonishing tribute to his local standing. 'A number of mutes, undertakers, etc., preceded a hearse decked with plumes and drawn by six horses. After the hearse came eight stage-coaches and four. Then followed fifteen post-chaises, conveying innkeepers and other friends of the deceased, and the procession closed with six mail guards in uniform and 160 horsemen, two and two. An immense crowd lined St Sidwell's as far as St Ann's Chapel.' And with the funeral procession of this famous character we may take our farewell of Georgian Exeter.

57   The *New London Inn* c.1870.

58   The High Street and the Guildhall *c.*1830.

CHAPTER EIGHT

The Early Nineteenth Century

Smells and Culture

WHAT DID THE CITY OF EXETER look like in the early 19th century? It all depends whether one was a visitor just passing through, or whether one lived here. And those who lived here saw it in quite different ways, depending on whether they were well-to-do people living on Southernhay or Pennsylvania or labourers living in the West Quarter.

To Robert Southey the poet, who visited us in September 1799, Exeter was an old-fashioned and smelly place, but with some fine features. He stayed at the *New London Inn*, which had been built only five years earlier by John Land the innkeeper, 'an inn as large as a convent'. He asked if it was possible for such an immense house ever to be filled by travellers and was told that there were two others in the city nearly as large,* besides many smaller inns, and that it was sometimes impossible to find a bed anywhere except in a private house. The luxury of the interior of the *New London* also impressed him. This fine inn was used all through the 19th century for official and ceremonial banquets, but was demolished in 1930 to make way for the Savoy cinema (later the A.B.C. cinema).

Southey goes on to say that

> Exeter is an ancient city, and has been so slow in adopting modern improvements that it has the unsavoury odour of Lisbon. One great street runs through the city from east to west; the rest consists of dirty lanes … The streets are not flagged, neither are they regularly cleaned as in other parts of the kingdom; the corporation used to compel the townspeople to keep their doors clean as is usual in every English town; but some little while ago it was discovered that, by the laws of the city, they had no authority to insist upon this; and now the people will not remove the dirt from their own doors, because they say they cannot be forced to do it.

It was a by-law as far back as the 16th century that citizens should keep clean the street in front of their own property, but this requirement had apparently lapsed. In September 1800 another by-law was made requiring people to sweep the pavement in front of their houses three times a week, and scavengers were appointed by the city to collect the sweepings. For

---

* These two would have been the *Half Moon* and the *Royal Clarence* (then simply known as *The Hotel*).

59 The opening of Rougemont House and Gardens, 2 April 1912.

a time the streets were vastly improved, but within a couple of years everything was as bad again. Much depended on the activity and personal interest of the mayor, and a lazy or indifferent mayor soon produced a lazy administration.

Exeter was old-fashioned also: people still called the Americans 'the rebels' though the war of American Independence had ended nearly twenty years earlier. Joseph Priestley, who was chiefly known in his day as a defender of the French Revolution, was regarded in Exeter as the devil himself. When he was in the city, and was being shaved by a barber, the latter—on hearing who his customer was—dropped his razor immediately (perhaps fortunately) and rushed out of the room saying that 'he had seen his cloven foot'.

Still, there were things to admire in the city. The cathedral was 'a noble pile' and Northernhay, where the elms planted long ago by the city fathers had now reached their full growth, was thought by Southey to be the finest public walk he had seen. Northernhay had been levelled in 1612 and made into a pleasant grassy walk among the trees, with seats at intervals, all at the city's expense. It is still one of the most attractive features of Exeter. Southey also saw the gardens which had been made in the castle ditch, known to us as Rougemont Gardens, and greatly admired them. Mr John Patch, a distinguished surgeon at the Devon and Exeter Hospital, had leased the site from the Duchy of Cornwall and had built a mansion here (now

Rougemont House), about 1769-70.* After his death in 1787 the property passed to Edmund Granger, the wine merchant, who altered and improved the house and gardens with the help and advice of William Jackson. The house became the city reference library until 1966, then a museum of local history, costume and lace, and lately a resource centre for schools; the gardens, with their superb trees, remain pretty much as Southey saw them. The house and gardens were acquired by the city in 1912.

Exeter, for all its smells and general backwardness, was very much the provincial capital with the amenities of a learned and cultivated society. Southey calls William Jackson 'one of the most accomplished men of his age ... chiefly celebrated as a musician; but as a man of letters his reputation is considerable; and he was also a painter: few men, if any, have succeeded so well in so many of the fine arts'. He was organist of Exeter cathedral, friend of the eminent in London to whom he was known as 'Jackson of Exeter', and composed operas, one of which was staged at Drury Lane. But Jackson was only one of many distinguished men living in Exeter at this time.

There had been a literary society in the city until the French Revolution broke it up, probably by stifling the free discussion between learned and urbane men which is the life-blood of any cultivated society. But the city possessed the finest collection of books for sale anywhere outside London, brought together by Gilbert Dyer whom Southey called 'a thinking, extraordinary man, of liberal and extraordinary talents for his circumstances'. Dyer died in October 1820, having lived to see the foundation of the Devon and Exeter Institution (1813) as a learned library and society.

A New Kind of City

Exeter was changing its character rapidly in the first forty years of the 19th century. Down to the outbreak of the French Wars (1793) she had still been an important industrial and commercial city, with a very considerable overseas trade; but the twenty or more years of war and blockade had practically killed all this trade. Despite this heavy blow, the city doubled in size between 1800 and 1840. Why was this?

At the beginning of the century Exeter, with its mainly working-class suburb of St Thomas across the river, had just about 20,000 people. Heavitree was still a pleasant little village of a few hundred people to which middle-class citizens who could afford it migrated for a summer holiday and the salubrious country air. The suburb of St Leonard's had not yet come into existence. By the 1840s, the population of the city and its suburbs had increased to some 40,000. Heavitree was now joined to Exeter, not continuously but by large houses in ample gardens, and the suburb of St Leonard's, largely occupied by the families of naval and military men, had come into existence since 1830. It was developed mainly by the big building family of Hooper who bought much of the Baring estate on this side of Exeter in the 1820s.

* Mr. Patch took a lease of the site in 1768.

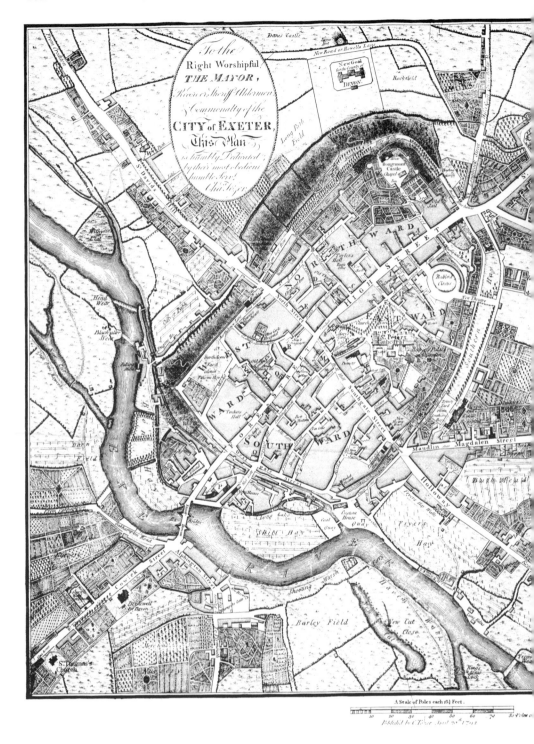

60 Exeter in 1792, surveyed by Charles Tozer.

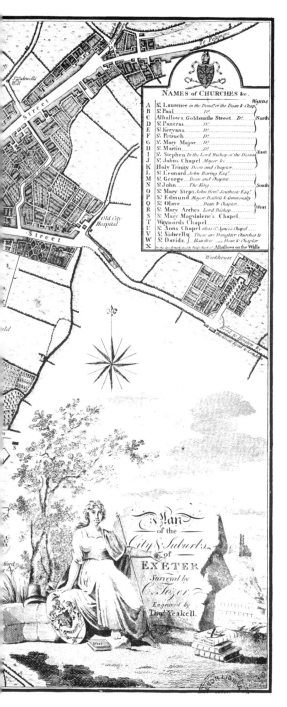

NAMES of CHURCHES &c.

		WARDS
A	S.<sup> Laurence in the Donet of the Doan & Chap.	
B	S.<sup> Paul	D.<sup>
C	Alhallows Goldsmith Street	D.<sup> North
D	S.<sup> Pancras	D.<sup>
E	S.<sup> Kervans	D.<sup>
F	S.<sup> Petrock	D.<sup>
G	S.<sup> Mary Major	D.<sup>
H	S.<sup> Martin	D.<sup>
I	S.<sup> Stephen In the Lord Bishop of the Diocese East
J	S.<sup> Johns Chapel Mayor &c.
K	Holy Trinity Dean and Chapter
L	S.<sup> Leonard John Baring Esq.<sup>
M	S.<sup> George Dean and Chapter
N	S.<sup> John The King South
O	S.<sup> Mary Steps John Hen.<sup> Southcote Esq.<sup>
P	S.<sup> Edmund Mayor Bailies & commonalty
Q	S.<sup> Olave Dean & Chapter West
R	S.<sup> Mary Arches Lord Bishop
S	S.<sup> Mary Magdalene's Chapel
T	Waynards Chapel
U	S.<sup> Anns Chapel alias S.<sup> Agnes' Chapel
V	S.<sup> Sidwells These are Daughter Churches to
W	S.<sup> Davids. These are Dean & Chapter
X	Alhallows on the Walls

The climate, amenities, and scenery of Exeter were attracting well-to-do families from all over the country just at the time when its ancient industries and trades were dying. These newcomers needed good houses, services of all kinds, and more shops of all sorts. So followed a great expansion of the building industry to take the obvious point first. In 1801 there were 2,836 houses within the old city limits, or 3,278 including St Thomas. In 1841 the old city had 5,639 houses, and the three suburbs some 1,700 houses between them. Altogether, nearly four thousand new houses were built in and immediately around the city in the space of forty years. This may not seem a large number by modern standards (which are abnormal) but to the city of those days it was a phenomenal rate of growth. Not only all this house-building activity, but major public works going on all the time—new roads and streets everywhere, new markets, new prisons, new baths and other public buildings, new churches.

Exeter was a rich little city. Its once-flourishing woollen industry, and other less-known but profitable industries like banking, brewing, and tanning, had produced a comparatively large class of 'unearned income' receivers. And the large class of retired people from other parts were in the main well-to-do, and brought a great deal of money into the city from outside. Most of the houses built in these years were large or at least comfortable villas. The large and handsome houses which still stand in Baring Crescent were styled 'superior cottages' when they were begun in 1818.

The principal builders in Exeter at this date were William Hooper and Matthew Nosworthy, both of whom left their mark upon the finest parts of the city. They made it notable among English towns for its dignified late Georgian building. They were their own architects, and splendid ones they were, too. Much of their work is now gone, some destroyed by the Germans in 1942 and some in later years by an insensitive city council. One of the finest crescents still remaining is Barnfield Crescent, begun by Nosworthy in 1792. Dix's Field was also by Nosworthy, begun about 1810 but now largely destroyed. Colleton Crescent was begun by Nosworthy in 1802 on a magnificent site overlooking the river and the canal. It was painted by J.M.W. Turner in a well-known picture, and remains for our pleasure today. Nosworthy also built many of the terrace houses in Southernhay, which was created between about 1798 and 1820.

William Hooper built Higher Summerlands (from 1804 onwards: destroyed in 1942), Lower Summerlands (1814 onwards: still standing), Baring Place (1808 onwards), Chichester Place (in Southernhay, 1824-5:

61 Colleton Crescent.

62 Southernhay West.

a fine colonnaded group), and much of St Leonard's Road (from 1828 onwards). The full catalogue of buildings by Hooper and Nosworthy has yet to be made, but one recognises their urbane building all over Exeter and its inner suburbs. Another magnificent terrace was Pennsylvania Park (1822-3), built by Brown, perhaps the finest domestic architecture of any in Exeter. But scattered all over Exeter are little Regency and Greek Revival villas, in unexpected places, shaded by ilex trees or magnolias. The earlier buildings were in the local blood-red brick; the later ones generally stuccoed and painted white. And of the public buildings of the period, far above all (and many were very good) stands the monumental Higher Market in Queen Street, designed by Charles Fowler (an Exeter-born architect) and built by the Hoopers, who seem to have secured most of the public building of this period. It was opened in 1838. The Lower Market—destroyed in

63   The Higher Market.

the war—was also by Fowler, and was a superb classical building. It stood in its ruin after 1942 like a piece of ancient Rome: indeed one could imagine oneself among the ruined public buildings of the fifth century in Exeter. Charles Fowler built a great deal in London, but it was for his native city that he reserved his masterpiece—the Higher Market, one of the noblest buildings in the West of England. The interior, with its clerestoried and granite-pillared hall, is also magnificent. The entire Market has been integrated into the Guildhall Shopping Precinct.

The new houses of these years of elegance needed large staffs of servants to run them, many shops to feed and supply them, many artisans to service them, many clergy, lawyers, and doctors to minister to them. It was around this core of a large, comfortable, middle class that the new kind of Exeter developed during the 19th century.

64 Rear of the Higher Market before the ground level was raised for the Guildhall Shopping Centre.

65 The Lower Market.

When Richard Ford, the celebrated author of the *Handbook for Travellers in Spain*, was looking round for a house on his return from a long residence in Spain, he eventually chose Exeter as the best of all English towns in which to live. He took a house on Southernhay while looking for a suitable house to buy. From there he wrote to his friend Henry Addington:

> This Exeter is quite a capital, abounding in all that London has, except its fog and smoke. There is an excellent institution here with a well-chosen large Library. the Devon and Exeter Institution, in which I take great pastime and am beginning my education. There is a bookseller who has some *ten thousand* old tomes to tempt a poor man. However, here one has no vices or expenses except eating clotted cream, and a *duro* crown piece wears a hole in your pocket before you are tempted to change it.

A few months later, still not settled on a house, he writes:

> There are houses of all sorts from £50 a year to £250; one at that price is beautiful and fit for a Plenipo ... The women, God be praised! are very ugly. Meat at 6d. a pound, butter seldom making 1s ... A Mr. Radford, who has a place to sell, has one gardener, who looks after two acres and three horses, all for a matter of £15 or so a year. Servants go twice to church of a Sunday, and masters read family prayers, and make them work their bodies like galley slaves, *per contra* the benefit conferred on their souls.
>
> The town is ... quiet and literary: clergymen, physicians, colonels, plain £1,000-a-year folk, given to talk about quarter sessions and the new road bill (if you will allow them). Otherwise a man goes quietly down hill here, *oblitus et obliviscendus*, reads his books (or those of the Institution), goes to church, and gets rich, which is a very pleasurable and a novel feeling—better than the *romance* of youth.

Richard Ford eventually bought Heavitree House and spent a great deal of money on doing it up in a Victorian Gothic style, and in laying out gardens in the Moorish fashion. And it was here, in a myrtle-covered garden-house, on an ink-stained deal table, that he wrote his famous *Handbook for Travellers in Spain* in the years between 1840 and 1845, the most famous book ever written in Exeter. Ford's letters are full of the delights of living in Exeter, and above all in his house at Heavitree.* But it is time to look at another kind of Exeter which never came his way and which he would never have dreamt of noticing—the Exeter of the working class, of the vast majority of the citizens.

The Working Class

The greater part of the population of the city consisted of small shopkeepers, artisans of various kinds but mainly in the building trades, and labourers. About 1820 craftsmen in the building trades were able to earn about 2s. 8d. a day, or 16s. a week when in full employment.

* This house, Old Heavitree House, has now (1960) been demolished and its once beautiful gardens have been 'developed' for building.

Labourers got 2s. 2d. a day, or 13s. in a full week. But building was the chanciest of all trades. There was no lack of employment in the city in these decades of building everywhere, but bad weather could stop work for a week on end at times. Wages rose slowly in those days, but by the early 'thirties master craftsmen could earn 3s. 4d. a day, or 21s. a week at the best, and labourers were getting 2s. 4d. a day or 14s. in a full week. These rates had not changed twenty years later.

Trade unions have never been very strong in this part of England. As early as 1834 an attempt was made to form a trade union in the building trades, chiefly among the bricklayers, instigated by two delegates from the central union in London. The *Flying Post* (a Conservative paper) reported at length in January of that year on an extraordinary affair at the *Sun Inn*, which formerly stood in Sun Street (between South Street and Preston Street). Reading it all now it has a slightly comic element about it, but at the time it was a matter almost of life and death.

It became known to the authorities that two men—James Stoddart and Daniel Gill—had arrived in the city from London with the object of forming a trade union in Exeter. Their presence had also become known to many journeymen, especially to the bricklayers and masons with whom meetings had been secretly held, accompanied it was said by 'nonsensical mummery and unlawful oaths'. It became known to the mayor that 'assemblages of a secret kind' were taking place, and the attention of the police was drawn to Stoddart and Gill. Howard and Taylor, captains of the watch, were particularly on the alert. The former had learnt that on the evening of Wednesday, 15 January, a secret meeting was to be held at the *Sun*. The mayor informed his fellow magistrates, and the whole police force was alerted. On the night of the meeting the watchful Howard entered the *Sun Inn*, took possession of a room next to that in which he surmised the meeting was to be held, and bored a hole in the thin partition between the rooms. All this was presumably done with the connivance of the landlord who had probably been warned and terrorised, but we are not told this. About fifty or sixty men assembled in the meeting-room, and the grotesque ceremony of initiating new members began. It should be said that since trade unions were suspect activities at this date, the early unions often went in for these rather ludicrous secret initiation ceremonies which a more enlightened administration would have quietly ignored.

At this exciting point, the redoubtable Howard shinned down from a window, raced to the Guildhall where the police were waiting under Captain Cuthberton, and the whole crowd—the police captain and his 'corps of constables', the four captains of the watch, and sundry reinforcements—proceeded to the scene of the crime, if crime it was. The stairs were rushed, but the door of the meeting-room was guarded by a hefty workman. He was swept out of the way, but the door-handle was fixed on the inside. The police crashed against the door. Fifty bricklayers and masons were wedged against it on the other side. Hell was let loose, but it was nothing to what was to come. After several minutes of titanic heaving on both sides, the police got into the room. Immediately all the lights in the room went out, all except one candle which was seized by a tall constable and held above his head to direct operations. Then the solitary candle was knocked flying, and in the blackness of a January night men leapt from windows as fast as they could. But it took a long time to empty a room so crowded, lights were fetched, the exits barred, and eventually nearly forty men were made prisoner.

'On a table in the room', says the *Flying Post*, trying to frighten its comfortable middle-class readers (of whom Richard Ford was no doubt one), 'lay the Bible open, and a Testament, a manuscript book of proceedings, the oath of initiation, letters, papers, etc. There were also formed of wood, sundry representations of ancient battle axes and two swords.' Besides all this there were two masks, hoods of sheepskin like judges' wigs, and two flowing white garments like surplices. Over all was a gaunt figure of Death painted on canvas about six or seven feet high, with right arm raised and the hand holding a dart with which it appeared to be about to transfix the person before it. Above this ghastly figure was an inscription: *Remember thy latter end*. When the police burst in on that memorable scene, three men were standing blindfolded. The old ladies of Exeter, reading this stuff, had their massive prejudices against trade unions amply confirmed.

By now it was late at night, but the mayor and Alderman Sanders, the banker, were sitting at the Guildhall waiting for the criminals to be brought in. The proceedings went on for three or four hours. The Press were told not to report any of the evidence. Eventually, all but 15 of the prisoners were released. All the prisoners, except the two London delegates, were said to be bricklayers in good employment. The two London men looked like 'decent mechanics in their Sunday clothes. They are from London, and from certain documents found in the pockets of one of them, though now enriched and enabled to travel and live at their ease from the funds formed by the contributions of infatuated and deluded men, their own circumstances must have been anything rather than good.' The magistrates conducted their second examination in the secrecy of the prison, much to the annoyance of the Press (which to their credit did not approve of these attempts to shut them up). It was decided to send all 15 prisoners to the next assizes on a charge of 'combining and confederating themselves together for the purpose of effecting an unlawful object'. All were allowed bail, though the sums were fixed high.

The assizes took place in late July, and the sequel is astonishing when one remembers the frightened temper of these years. In March six Dorset farm-workers had been sentenced to transportation for seven years at the Dorchester assizes for precisely the same offence as the Exeter bricklayers were alleged to have committed. Trade unions had been legalised in 1825 but their rapid growth in the 'thirties alarmed some of the more backward magistrates who made use of an act prohibiting 'unlawful oaths' in order to suppress them where they could. Despite the great outcry against the monstrous sentence on the Tolpuddle labourers, they were duly shipped to Australia. The Prime Minister at this time was the unspeakable Lord Melbourne.

The Exeter bricklayers and the two London men were tried before the Lord Chief Justice (Denman). They were defended by Mr Serjeant Wilde who said forthwith he could not defend their conduct. 'The object of those who originated the Prosecution was to show the working classes that such acts would not be permitted. The parties had made a most unreserved acknowledgement of the illegality of their proceedings.' They were accordingly found guilty, but then were bound over and set free. They had had a merciful escape: but perhaps the government itself was not unalarmed at the public reaction to the Dorchester sentences; and the Exeter bricklayers, suitably frightened, were allowed to go home again. Almost thirty years went by before another attempt was made, this time successfully, to form a trade union. On 16 March 1862 the Exeter Lodge of the Operative Bricklayers' Society was opened, probably at the *Britannia Inn* in South Street, where it continued to meet for many years until it moved to the *Valiant Soldier* at the corner of Magdalen Street.

The law was equally savage against offences relating to private property. The Gaol Books of the so-called House of Correction (which stood where the *Rougemont Hotel* now is) show what things were like in the year 1830 for example. This prison had been built in 1818 to replace the ancient city prison in the South Gate, one of the foulest holes in England. But the new House of Correction was not much better. It had a tread-wheel with machinery for the purpose of beating hemp, and the cells were grossly overcrowded. In some no fewer than six prisoners slept. They had, indeed, been built to accommodate several prisoners, 'a plan never pursued at the best gaols'.

The House of Correction (what an ironic name!) was chiefly occupied by 'vagrants', who were usually sentenced to one or two months' hard labour. The next largest class of 'criminal' was the bad apprentice. William Rouse, aged 17, convicted of being a bad apprentice, was sentenced to 14 days at the tread-wheel and flogged at the end of the sentence. Edward Ley, aged 15, served two months in this prison for stealing apples. A boy of 14, described as a vagrant, was sentenced to one month at the tread-wheel, a vagrant girl of 14 to two months' hard labour. Her behaviour in prison was described as 'bad'. These children were housed with prostitutes, of whom there seem to have been a great number in early Victorian Exeter, a product for the most part of the frightful poverty of the 'West Quarter'.

But the great majority of working-class people in Exeter never had to face the magistrates or the judges (fortunately for them, for the Bench seems to have been mostly filled with unconscious sadists), and there were pleasanter things in life for a good workman who did not fall upon bad times. There were, for example, the annual outings of the various firms. The *Flying Post* reports (8 September 1836):

> On Saturday last, according to annual custom, the workmen in the employ of Messrs. S. & W. Kingdon, of this city, the most extensive ironmongers and founders in the West of England, marched in procession through the city accompanied by the Moreton band, and with numerous banners etc. to Heavitree, where they were treated by their liberal employers to a well supplied and substantial dinner.

The coachmakers employed by Messrs Hayman and Son went as far afield as the *Rolle Arms* at Budleigh Salterton for their feast, no doubt in one of their own coaches; and the employees of Mr William Cooke,

66 Tuckers Hall, originally the 15th-century chapel of the Guild of Weavers, Fullers and Shearmen, converted to their meeting room in the 17th century.

saddler, coach and harness maker, dined together at the *Huntsman Inn* at Ide, 'the dinner being substantial and well served, and the afternoon spent with great harmony'.

The most charming of all was the annual celebration of the tuckers (or fullers) and shearmen in the early part of the 19th century. This took place at the *Windmill Inn*, which formerly stood on the lower corner of Holloway Street and Bull Meadow Road.* Many of them found employment in this district in what was the Larkbeare establishment of Mr Charles Bowring. Their great day was 'Nutting Day', the last Thursday in August. First came a good lunch at the *Windmill*, which was noted for the quality of its home-brewed ale. Then the whole party went out gathering nuts in the fields and copses which were then not far away; and having nutted to their heart's content they returned to the *Windmill* for dinner. This was frequently presided over by Mr Charles Bowring. Here the company ate, drank, and sang the evening hours away, the oldest member obliging with a parody of 'The Vicar of Bray', with the chorus

> And this is law I will maintain
> Until my dying day, sir:
> Let whatever King shall reign,
> I'll drink my gallon a day, sir.

* The *Windmill*'s licence lapsed in August 1885 and the site is now covered with small houses.

The day was a customary holiday. Flags were displayed inside and outside the inn, and young trees planted every year in the road. As members of a guild, the holiday-makers wore emblematic aprons, the fullers having a green apron with white serge strings, and the dyers a blue apron with red serge strings.

Besides the regular patronage of the serge-makers, the *Windmill* enjoyed the custom of Topsham people engaged in the fish trade. Before the railway was built (in 1861) some 15 carts were regularly employed in bringing fish into the city from Topsham, half-a-dozen of them being usually drawn up outside the *Windmill* at any given time. Public-houses kept open then all day long.* The directory for 1850 shows that there were no fewer than 148 hotels, inns, and taverns in a city which, with its small suburbs, contained no more than 40,000 people. There were nearly forty hostelries within two hundred yards of the centre of the city.

Among the notable customers of the old *Windmill* was the great tragedian Edmund Kean, who first rose to fame by his acting on the Exeter stage. It was in this city that Kean perfected his art, first appearing with his wife in *The Mountaineers* on 2 December 1811. The next night he played in his great role of Shylock, to unbounded applause, and was thereupon engaged by the manager of the theatre for three years at a salary of two guineas a week. He remained in Exeter until April 1813, playing many Shakespearian parts and also in Pantomime.

Poor Kean, who had had a fearfully hard life, was already a heavy drinker in his early twenties. One old Exeter citizen in the 1880s recalled seeing him between five and six o'clock in the morning, staggering along the street clad in the costume of Richard III, which he had played the night before. Often he had to be fetched at the last moment from a neighbouring inn and doused with cold water before he could go on the stage. Once he appeared on the stage in a manifestly unsteady condition. Some of the audience hissed, and Kean, stung by the demonstration, pulled himself together and played his part magnificently.

But in April 1813 he went too far. He turned up at the theatre much the worse for drink, so much so that Mr Hughes, the manager, had to take over Kean's part. During the performance, Kean took possession of a private box, and at the most inappropriate moments shouted in his mocking, searching voice, 'Bravo! Hughes!' That was the last straw. The great tragedian received his dismissal. With his son Howard at his side, and his wife carrying the infant Charles in her arms, Kean trudged all the way to Dorchester to find fresh employment. In less than a year he had made his triumphant debut as Shylock at Drury Lane. When we walk along the prosaic pavement of Holloway Street today we may well recall the reeling figure of England's greatest tragic actor, on his way home from the *Windmill* in the early hours, 200 years ago. The streets of Exeter are peopled with ghosts, if we know where to look for them.

---

* The new Licensing Act, which compelled public houses to close at 11 p.m., provoked serious riots in Exeter for several nights in August 1872.

The Cholera Epidemic

There had always been great poverty in Exeter, which probably reached its worst during the 19th century. There was the Workhouse, it is true, but most of the poor resented and feared this institution. Besides this a number of voluntary societies had grown up in the city to relieve poverty of various kinds. No fewer than eight of these societies were founded between 1799 and 1833. The oldest of them was the Society for the Relief of the Sober and Industrious Poor, which sold coal at reduced prices to deserving families. During the winter of 1836-7, for instance, it sold some 350 tons at 1d. for 20 lbs, or about 5½d. a hundredweight. The latest of these societies was the Exeter Clothing Society, established to supply the poorer classes with useful clothing at reduced prices and to employ 'individuals of the same description' in making up the clothing.

We get some idea of the abysmal poverty of the West Quarter of Exeter from the pages of Dr Shapter's book, *History of the Cholera in Exeter*. The most overcrowded parishes at this time (1832) were St Mary Major, St Mary Steps, and St George, all of which had an average of more than two families to every house. Several other parishes were nearly as bad, such as St Olave and St Mary Arches, which had been rich parishes in the 16th century. In all these parishes which had once been rich, the large merchants' houses had been cut up into tenements housing two, three, or more families, and the ample gardens and courtyards of the old houses had been seized upon by speculative builders for rows of cottages crammed together and reached by means of a covered passage rather like a tunnel. Older Exonians will remember these slum courts in various parts of the city, now almost entirely swept away. By building on all the open spaces that were available, the rapidly rising population of the city in the early 19th century was housed in one way or another.

67 John Gendall's drawing of a cholera victim's coffin being carried along Goldsmith Street.

In this crowded city of narrow streets, practically no sewers existed in the year of the cholera. Some of the principal streets occupied by the wealthier citizens had recently been given sewers (High Street was given a sewer in 1807, which may have been the first in Exeter) but over most of the city the only means for removing household and trade filth was by the open gutters or 'cannels' in the middle of the streets. Much of the city had no adequate water supply, which made cleanliness even more difficult.

The cholera, hitherto unknown in England, slowly crept across Europe. By June 1831 it had reached Hamburg, and soon had crossed the North Sea to Gateshead and Sunderland. The authorities at first denied that it was cholera, and the citizens of Exeter were inclined to ignore it as having a disturbing effect on business. But the authorities began to take some elementary precautions during the autumn. The cholera reached London on 13 February 1832; by mid-July it was reported from Plymouth and it was clear that Exeter could not hope to escape. On 19 July the first case was reported in the city. A woman in North Street, who had just come from Plymouth, died of it within a few hours. Within a week the number of burials in the Bartholomew Yard was creating alarm and burial grounds had to be found outside the city in order to allay public feeling. One of these was Bury Meadow.

As the weeks went by the streets were almost deserted except for the frequent funerals, and the only sound was that of the tolling of church bells. This melancholy sound so preyed upon the minds of the living that it was eventually stopped. The turning-point was reached about 22 August and the visitation finally ended in the latter part of September. Altogether 402 people had died of the disease in Exeter itself, and another 38 in St Thomas, 440 deaths in all. On 10 October a General Thanksgiving was held at which the Bishop (Philpotts) preached. He had absented himself from the city all the time the cholera had raged, a fact that was never afterwards forgotten. But the medical profession had behaved heroically all through these terrible weeks, and on 22 October a public meeting was called to show the general appreciation of their services. As a result of this epidemic the water supply of the city was vastly improved, some of the worst slums were pulled down, and 13 miles of sewers were laid in the streets which had had none before. The whole city was sewered at a cost of nearly £80,000. Among many changes, the Longbrook on the north of the city, and the Shitbrook on the south, were covered in (in 1843) and used as storm-sewers.* But these ancient streams still run far under ground, and find their way as of old through darkness into the river Exe.

These streams had been used as open drains for centuries, and were foul in dry or hot weather. But they were probably not as beastly as we might think. Old citizens thought of them with affection. Edward Ashworth, the Exeter architect, who died in 1896, recalled the Long Brook flowing from Lions Holt as an open running stream at the bottom of Longbrook Street, separating the then little village of Hill's Court from Exeter. The brook was crossed here by a wooden bridge and 'white posts with overhanging willow trees marked the course of the sparkling stream'. A footpath followed the stream to the old St David's church. This was a favourite Sunday afternoon walk, so it could not have been so bad after all.

* The Improvement Commissioners met in late August 1832 and ordered 'an open sewer' at the bottom of Longbrook Street to be covered forthwith. The Chamber declined to do this, but in May 1843 the Improvement Commissioners resolved that all uncovered drains should be covered, including the Longbrook and the Shitbrook. The work seems to have been done soon afterwards.

CHAPTER NINE

Victorian Exeter

Mostly about Money

DOWN TO 1835 the city of Exeter was governed by a self-elected corporation known as the Chamber. Including the mayor there were eight aldermen and 16 common councillors. The old unreformed corporations were the subject of a full-scale government enquiry in 1835. Some of them were on the whole well managed corporations but that of Exeter, though by no means the worst, did not come well out of the scrutiny. Besides being self-elected and filling vacancies privately, the Chamber held their meetings in private with the result that

> they have not gained the confidence of the inhabitants. It is true there has been no appropriation of the funds of the corporation to the purposes of individual members of the body ... but the corporation have not administered the public property with prudence or discretion, whilst their misappropriation to corporate purposes of the funds for which they were trustees for charities, subjects them to serious reproach. With an ample income for public purposes, under an economical but liberal expenditure, sufficient for all the objects of municipal government, they have been constantly increasing the corporate debt. The expenditure on the canal has been most improvident: a debt of more than £100,000 has been incurred on this account alone ... for the misappropriation of the charity funds the present members of the corporation are not accountable, and at this time the management of the charities appears to be very excellent; but the impropriety of contracting a vast share of the overwhelming debt of the corporation belongs to the present body.

At this time the city income was about £11,000 a year. Of this sum some £8,000 came from canal dues and quay and town dues.* The remainder came from the rents of property and from market tolls.

Most of the expenditure of the city went on the canal, especially the heavy burden of interest on the canal debt. Apart from this the bulk of the money was spent on the police and on the gaol. The Chamber therefore had a very limited income and very limited functions. The important tasks

---

* Compare this with three hundred years earlier. In the 1540s the total income of the city was about £250 a year, the average annual expenditure £227. By the 1630s the city was spending nearly £1,100 a year and there was a floating debt of about £1,500.

of paving, lighting, cleaning, and otherwise improving the city, were left
to a specially appointed body—the Improvement Commissioners—who had
been set up in 1810 and whose functions were not taken over by the city
council until 1864. There were very few city officials. Local government
was in a rudimentary state. In 1840, for example, there were only four
chief officers, the town clerk and the treasurer, whose salaries were £200
a year each, the surveyor who got £150 a year, and the superintendent of
police who got £120.

By the end of the century the city was receiving and spending just
over £30,000 a year. In 1900-1 the borough rate produced nearly half the
total income of the city council, and most of the rest came from the
central exchequer. There were now a few more officials. The town clerk
had risen to £765 a year, the city surveyor to £600, and the city treasurer
to £496, out of which he had to provide his own offices and clerks. The
chief constable earned £270 a year plus £10 allowance in lieu of uniform,
and the electrical engineer £275. There was also the superintendent of the
fire brigade, who got £150 a year.

As for expenditure, it was—apart from interest on the city debt—mostly
going on education and the police, with a small amount on the canal.

Exeter Politics

When the new council was elected at the end of 1835, and the old Chamber
abolished, the city was overwhelmingly Liberal in its sentiments (or so
it was said). The Liberals agreed, however, to share the representation on
the new council half and half with the Conservatives (18 members each).
But the Liberals had elected as councillor a Quaker who refused to qualify
himself for office, so that they found themselves in a minority of one at
the election of the 12 aldermen. With this unexpected tactical advantage,
the Conservatives snatched 11 of the aldermanic seats, the 12th going to
Mr William Kennaway, a Liberal, only because his was the first name to be
called. So the new council started with a Conservative majority of 11, and
elected as mayor Mr Samuel Kingdon, a Tory Unitarian. This unprincipled
coup enabled the Tories to work the new Corporation in their own interest,
turning out all the old officers as far as they could, and it also enabled them
to keep out of the mayoralty for life Mr Mark Kennaway, one of the ablest
Liberals in the city. The moral of this tale is: never trust any party politician
of any colour: children cannot learn this lesson too soon in life.

Though the Liberals asserted that the city was overwhelmingly disposed
towards them, the parliamentary elections of the following generation do
not bear them out. Exeter had always returned two members of Parliament.
In 1832 both were Liberals, but from 1835 to 1868 the representation was
almost invariably shared between the two parties. Altogether 13 Liberals
were elected, as against 12 Conservatives.

From 1868 to 1873 the city was represented by two Liberals, but then
the tide slowly turned. In the election of 1874 the city returned both
members as Conservatives, reverting to one of each in 1880-5. When Exeter
was reduced to one member in 1885, the sentiment of the city became

markedly Conservative for the next 22 years. Until the fateful year of 1906, Exeter was represented without a break by a Tory. Yet the Tory majority was rarely more than a few hundred in a total poll of six or seven thousand. When Sir George Kekewich captured the city for the Liberals in the fierce election of 1906, in which hundreds of Conservative members all over the kingdom lost their seats, his majority was less than one hundred in a poll of nearly nine thousand.

Exeter was in fact, from 1832 onwards, pretty well evenly divided between the two parties. In the first election of 1910 Sir Henry Duke recaptured the city for the Conservatives (Unionists) with a majority of only twenty-six. In the second election at the end of the year the Liberal (R.H. St Maur) defeated Duke by four votes amid scenes of incredible excitement. The Conservatives petitioned for an enquiry into the voting and on a recount in April of the following year Sir Henry Duke was declared elected by one vote:

Henry Edward Duke (Unionist)	4,777
Richard Harold St Maur (Liberal)	4,776

Though the Conservatives represented Exeter in Parliament almost continuously from 1874 to 1914, except for a brief spell from 1906 to 1910, the city was in fact by no means so one-sided. For the best part of a hundred years it may be said to have been evenly split between the two parties. Only a minority of the adult population had a vote even in 1914: no woman could yet vote. And Exeter did not get its first Labour candidate until the general election of December 1923.

The Coming of the Railway

The first railway reached Exeter in May 1844, that from Bristol and London. But there might have been a line many years earlier, for as far back as 1825 there were meetings of influential people in Taunton and in Exeter for the purpose of initiating the construction of railroads. If the Taunton project had been realised, it would have linked Bristol and Exeter, and at Bristol links were envisaged with other railroads to London and the North.

The Exeter projects were far less ambitious, but it is remarkable enough to find Exonians so alive to the future of railways as early as this, at a time when only the Stockton and Darlington railway had proved its success as a commercial venture. Public meetings at Exeter discussed the making of a line from the Quay down to Powderham, where a dock was to be constructed near the church. Plans were actually prepared for this line, which still survive somewhere. There were other meetings to promote the construction of a line to Topsham and Exmouth.

These and other schemes fell through. In one of the early plans the main railway from Bristol was to sweep round the eastern side of Exeter and to have its main station in the Barnfield, and thence to run down to the Quay. Another plan was to bring the line along the eastern bank of the river, through Bonhay and across the foot of Bridge Street, across the Shilhay, over the river at Shooting Marsh, to terminate at the New Basin.

68 Exeter Quay *c.1835*: lithograph by W. Gauci after C.F. Williams.

The latter had been constructed by the city fathers in 1830 because natural impediments in the river-bed prevented the larger ships from reaching the old Quay. It was opened on 29 September in that year. A number of large barges were decorated with streamers and flags, and filled with ladies and gentlemen who, with guns firing and music playing, proceeded slowly down to Double Locks and back to the Basin amid the surrounding cheers of many thousand spectators who crowded the banks of the canal. Another great improvement of these years was the erection (in 1835) of the imposing warehouses on the Quay, which still survive among the more monumental architecture of old Exeter.

Within a few years the Bristol and Exeter Railway actually arrived, and the first train steamed into St David's station from Paddington on 1 May 1844 amid the cheers of a mighty throng who had poured into the city for hours on end that morning to see this latest achievement of modern science. When the railway was continued to Newton Abbot, it followed the western bank of the river, and not the line through Bonhay, and had a second station in the large suburb of St Thomas. By 1846 Exonians could travel by train to Dawlish, which rapidly became one of their favourite seaside resorts. Railway excursions began almost at once.

The first excursion train from London to Exeter arrived at St David's station about noon on 4 September 1844.

The next line to be completed was that from Exeter to Crediton, opened in 1851, and in 1860 came the second link with London with the completion of the railway from Yeovil to Exeter. The new line offered the prospect of competition for the Exeter-London traffic, and brought the city some twenty miles nearer the Metropolis, though the route was more severe. The opening day (18 July) was a general holiday in the city: most shops closed all day. The first train left Yeovil at noon and arrived at the Queen Street station in Exeter a few minutes after three o'clock, not a spectacular average speed but there had been congratulatory addresses at the principal stations all the way down. At four o'clock there was a Grand Banquet on Northernhay, overlooking the new railway, at which five hundred people feasted. The mayor presided and the chairman and other officers of the London and South Western Railway Company attended. For those who did not attend the banquet there was dancing in Bury Meadow at half past six that evening to the music of two bands. Our grandparents and great-grandparents seem strangely innocent and unsophisticated, dancing all the evening on the grass to celebrate the coming of another railway; but somehow railways have always seemed romantic. No one would feel impelled to dance to celebrate the arrival of a jet aircraft or a fleet of lorries. But Exeter retained this pleasant unsophistication until quite recent years, a capacity for the enjoyment of simple things which seems to have disappeared altogether from the world nowadays.

The coming of the L.& S.W.R. from Waterloo led immediately to the construction of the branch line from Exeter to Exmouth, opened in 1861 and talked about back in the 'twenties. In 1885 the charming little Exe Valley line was opened and, last of all, in 1903, the Teign Valley line was completed. Meanwhile the Crediton line had long before pushed on to Barnstaple (1854) and to Ilfracombe (1874), and all through the 1860s the railway was pressing forward slowly round the north of the Moor towards Plymouth. Okehampton was not reached until 1871. This second route from Exeter to Plymouth was not completed for another 20 years after this (1891).

Exeter was linked to Plymouth by the Great Western in 1848, and to Torquay (Torre) in the same year. By the 1870s we may say that the city had become a focal point for railways as she had been for many centuries for roads; and more and more Exeter men were finding secure employment 'on the railway'.

A Victorian Failure

On Saturday morning, 8 May, in the year 1869, the people of Exeter were staggered to hear that the sheriff of the city had died suddenly in London a few hours earlier at the age of forty-seven. He was Charles Wescomb, the owner of the leading Conservative newspaper in the city—the *Exeter and Plymouth Gazette*—and the mainspring of the Conservative party in Exeter. He not only owned the *Gazette* but he also owned three other newspapers, one in Kent, one in Edinburgh, and the London *Globe*. Besides owning these four newspapers in the Conservative interest he was the mainspring also of several mining and commercial undertakings and was regarded as one of the wealthiest of Exeter citizens.

He had been associated with nearly every public movement in Exeter for 12 years before his death and had sat on the council for St Sidwell's ward until he left Exeter for London early in 1867, in order to manage the *Globe* and to look after his other extensive interests. On his leaving Exeter, a great banquet was given in his honour at the *New London Hotel*, attended by political notabilities from the city and many parts of the county. Even after he had left Exeter he often returned to attend meetings and to record his vote. He was one of the originators of the School of Art and of the Albert Memorial Museum. When it was known he was contemplating a return to Exeter, he was chosen sheriff of the city (in November 1868) and there was every reason to suppose that within a few years he would become mayor.

Charles Wescomb was born in Paris Street in September 1821, the son of a bricklayer who worked for Messrs Hooper, the biggest builders in the city at this time. He was educated at St Sidwell's school, where he was a bright boy, especially at figures. The rector of St Sidwell's took an interest in him and at the age of 19 he was appointed schoolmaster at Budleigh Salterton at a salary of £30 a year and a house. He remained at Budleigh for 15 years and in 1855 returned to his native city. So far there had been nothing at all remarkable about his career, but in the next few years he succeeded in making a considerable fortune as an accountant speculating in mining shares. These were the boom years of the Devon and Cornish mines. We know nothing of the methods by which he made a fortune so quickly but his enemies frequently accused him of rigging mining shares in some unspecified way, his chief enemy being Thomas Latimer the owner and editor of the Liberal newspaper in the city, the *Western Times*.

When Mr Edward Woolmer, the owner of the *Exeter and Plymouth Gazette*, died in 1857, Charles Wescomb was called in as an accountant to deal with the winding-up of the estate. Within a year or two he succeeded in buying the *Gazette* from Woolmer's executors, and he also bought the substantial premises in the High Street (No. 229) where the *Gazette* had been carried on for a long period. In 1859 he was elected to the council, representing St Sidwell's ward, in which he had been born.

As the owner of the biggest Conservative newspaper in the city, he made himself the chief political guide of the Party. Meetings were held at his office in Gandy Street and nothing of importance was done without his advice and agreement. When cabinet ministers stayed at Pynes with Sir Stafford Northcote, Charles Wescomb was often invited out to meet the distinguished guests and to discuss the political management of the city.

Within the next few years he bought the *Maidstone Journal* and extended his political influence as far as Dover. He also bought the *Edinburgh Courant*, and a little later, the London *Globe*. All these newspapers he managed in the Conservative interest. Unknown to anyone but himself, however, he was by now in serious financial difficulties and he was borrowing wherever he could. It is likely that he had over-reached himself in his mining speculations and that the collapse of some of the Cornish mines in the 'sixties undermined what had once been a considerable fortune. All that was noticed in Exeter, on his frequent visits, was that his normally genial and sociable disposition had given way to prolonged periods of depression.

A few days before his death, he travelled down to Exeter and presided at a Trade Protection Society meeting. On the Tuesday afternoon he accompanied the mayor to Cowley Bridge with the intention of beating the bounds of the city, and on the Thursday afternoon—his last public engagement—he attended a meeting at the Guildhall at which the city council decided to adopt the Free Libraries Act and to found a public library in the city. He returned to London on Thursday night, had a stroke on the following day at noon, and died in the early hours of Saturday morning. He was buried at St Sidwell's church on 12 May 1869, in the presence of a large congregation, anxious to pay their last respects to a distinguished citizen who had risen from being a bricklayer's son to sheriff of his native city. On the following Sunday, many sermons were preached in the Exeter churches on the theme of his sudden death.

But within a week or two after this the dreadful revelations began. It was found that he had died bankrupt, owing money to all and sundry. The unfortunate rector of St Sidwell's was owed no less than £9,000 and there were other large creditors. But what was worse was that he had borrowed the life-savings of two or three aged widows who had been left completely destitute by his sudden death. On the very day of his election as sheriff he had borrowed nearly £100 from a Mrs Mary Chamberlain, and a widow Hooper had also lost all her savings.

It now appeared that all of Charles Wescomb's great ventures had been floated to a large extent on borrowed money. Prominent Conservatives like Sir Stafford Northcote had lent him money to purchase newspapers for the Conservative interest. His modest newspaper empire might well have succeeded, nevertheless, if his mining ventures had not come to grief. By the spring of 1869 he did not know where to turn for money to keep his numerous enterprises afloat, and it was revealed that his final stroke had been brought on as a result of an angry interview with someone in London whom he considered had let him down financially.

In order to suppress too much public scandal—and the *Western Times* was eager for every detail—Charles Wescomb's affairs were whisked into Chancery in London where they were gradually sorted out. His career is in its way a typical Victorian story: the poor boy who made good, who became a tycoon, who became intoxicated with his own apparent power in local politics, and who ran into financial difficulties in the end because he had no solid foundation on which to build. The revelations that followed his death, above all those characteristic figures the defrauded widows, stunned the local Conservatives, for he had been with them an immensely popular man, hospitable to a fault, and never better pleased than when he presided with friends around his own festive board. It took the Exeter Conservatives a very long time to get over the career of Charles Wescomb.

A Victorian Success Story

In the early 19th century the Willeys were all humble folk, small shopkeepers in St Sidwell's, boot and shoe makers, painters and glaziers. James Willey was a cordwainer, to use the old-fashioned word for a boot and shoe maker, living in Sidwell Street. To him and his wife Mary a son was born in late September of the year 1830, a son who was christened Henry Frederick at St Sidwell's church on 7 October of that year. From these humble beginnings, with no backing or influence of any sort, H.F. Willey founded the largest firm Exeter had ever seen—with over a thousand employees in its greatest years—became sheriff of the city at the age of 52, and mayor ten years later. Like most who come from lowly origins and rise in life, he was a strong Conservative all his life.

He was educated at St John's Hospital School, with what success we shall never know, as all the school records of these years were destroyed in the air-raids of 1942. From here he got a job at Vicary's, the gas-meter manufacturer and ironfounder. Mr Vicary died suddenly of a heart attack in the spring of 1868 (leaving a modest fortune of some £15,000). Willey was then nearing forty. He started the firm of Willey and Ford soon after this, possibly taking over Vicary's business on terms, but after a short while Mr Ford left the partnership (we know nothing of this inner history) and the business carried on as Willey & Co. The business thrived on gas-stoves and gas-meters; local politics took up more and more time; then civic honours came, culminating in the mayoralty of 1892-3. Late in February 1894 Henry Willey died, leaving a solid business and a respectable fortune of nearly £21,000.

So far the business, though a good one, was cramped on a small site in the Shilhay. Willey's eldest son—Henry Alfred—took it over at his father's death and made it the biggest firm in Exeter, indeed one of the largest engineering firms in the West of England. Though he lived only ten more years, dying of diabetes at the age of 41 in 1904, the younger Willey multiplied the family fortune five-fold in that short time. He left nearly £92,000, a large fortune for a city like Exeter.

He reorganised the firm completely. From the cramped quarters in Shilhay he removed the meter-makers to James Street and the other mechanics to new buildings near the Basin. When he was looking for a site for his new works, it was then a field with no road to it, he used to relate how he had to crawl through a gap in the hedge to prospect it. He acquired the rights in Mr Stephen Simpson's patents for making automatic gas-meters, which became a leading department of the firm. Soon the meter-department outgrew the James Street premises and was moved down to new buildings on the Basin site.

Although a confirmed Conservative like his father, he devoted himself entirely to the family business and took no part at all in public life, pursuing his fortune with all the characteristic energy of the diabetic. To the historian the Willeys are far less appealing than spectacular and colourful failures like Charles Wescomb; yet their prosaic success is a part of the story of Victorian Exeter and is worthy to be recorded. Like

69   Casting at Willey's Foundry on
18 April 1962.

70   Willey's coin-in-the-slot gas meter,
1947.

Charles Wescomb's story, they show
that it was possible for young men
of the humblest beginnings to rise
spectacularly even in supposedly
class-ridden Victorian days, where
there was enough native ability
and a single-minded devotedness to
making money—mercifully perhaps a rare quality among Exonians. Six
months after H. A. Willey's death there died an even richer and a worthier
citizen, Mr Edward Andrew Sanders, at the great age of ninety-two. He
was the grandson of Joseph Sanders, one of the founder partners of the
Exeter Bank, and was therefore the third generation of private bankers,
for the Bank was still a going concern at the time of his death. Edward
Sanders left the considerable fortune (in 1905) of just under £130,000. He
had been a political force in Exeter ever since 1835, and mayor as far back
as 1850. Dying in the reign of Edward VII, his long life had overlapped his
grandfather's by six years; and his grandfather could recall Exeter in the early
years of George II's reign. And if Grandfather Joseph Sanders ever spoke to
the young Edward of *his* father's days, the conversation would have taken
them back to the time of William and Mary, back to the greatest days

of the city's trade and prosperity. The Sanders family represented the Old Exeter, the Willeys the New.

Wages and Prices

In the year 1850 an Exeter labourer or navvy was getting 2s. 4d. a day, or 14s. a week if he worked a full week. Skilled craftsmen, such as carpenters or masons, could get 3s. a day, or 18s. in a full week. Hours of work were long. In the '60s men worked from six a.m. to half-past five in the evening, and to four o'clock on Saturdays. Conditions improved during the next forty years or so. Thus in the 1880s a craftsman in the building trades in Exeter could get 4½d. an hour, and he worked (if he was in full employment) ten hours a day for five days and eight hours on Saturdays, a total of 58 hours. It was about 1890 that Saturday work was reduced to six hours, stopping at one o'clock—a great step forward.*

By 1898 carpenters were getting 6d. an hour. With a 56 hour week this produced 28s. a week. Bricklayers got 6½d. an hour, labourers 4½d. A bricklayer could take home just over 29s. a week, but bad weather would reduce this appreciably.

The Exeter labourer about 1900 could earn 21s. a week in a full week. Carters were paid by the week, about 21s. a week for a seven-day week as they had to tend their horses on Sundays. At this time a policeman got 22s. 6d. a week on appointment, rising to 30s. a week after ten years' service; sergeants 32s. to 36s. (after five years), and inspectors 38s. to 44s. Even in 1912 a constable was getting only 24s. a week on appointment, rising to 31s. after ten years' service. On the other hand he had a uniform and other advantages, and it was pretty good pay for the period.

A linesman on the railway at the beginning of this century got 18s. a week. On the horse trams (which started in Exeter in 1882) a conductor started at 7s. a week, and drivers got 18s. or thereabouts. The electric trams started in 1905. Drivers started at 22s. 6d. a week, rising to 27s. after three or four years, conductors at 14s. The conductors' pay rose by 1s. a week for each year of service to a maximum of 18s.

It is simpler perhaps to show some of this information in the form of a table (see opposite).

On the whole wage-rates rose appreciably during the latter half of the 19th century and hours of work were considerably reduced. So by 1914 few men were doing more than a 54-hour week, though there were pockets of sweated labour: shop assistants and domestic servants as a class worked very long hours and were badly paid. In 1914 a housemaid could expect £24 a year, living in. Plain cooks could get £20 to £30 a year. Even here conditions had improved. An Exeter doctor's account book for 1843 shows that he was paying his two maids, Mary and Jane, £8 and £5 10s. a year respectively, while Alice (the cook?) got £12.

---

* I owe this and much of the following information to Mr Tom Neal, a retired master-builder who started as an employer in 1898.

Weekly Wages

	1850	1898	1903-4	1914
Labourer or navvy	14s.	21s.	22s. 6d.	24s. 9d.
Carpenter	21s.	28s.	33s. 9d.	36s.
Mason	21s.	—	36s.	38s. 3d.
Bricklayer	—	29s. 4d.	—	36s.
Road Sweeper	—	—	19s.	21s.
Carter	—	—	21s.	21s.
Plasterer	—	—	33s. 9d.	36s.
Plumber	—	—	33s. 9d.	36s.
Fitter	—	—	40s.	—
Smith	—	—	27s. 6d.	27s. 6d.
Policeman (on appt.)	16s.	22s. 6d.	—	24s.
Gardener	—	—	22s.	—
Shop Assistants				
Men	—	18s.	—	—
Girls	—	15s.	—	—
Clerks	—	22-25s.	—	—

The same account-book gives us an idea of the cost of living. He paid 'for Lucy's boots' 8s. 6d., and Lucy's bonnet cost no less than 35s. Lucy was his wife. The washerwoman's bill for the year was 12 guineas, so the whole family wash was done for a guinea a month. As a doctor, various people arrived at his door selling things. He records paying 2s. 9d. 'for a couple of ducks at the door'. On one occasion he bought a 5½lb. salmon at the door for half a crown, another couple of ducks for the same, a leg of lamb for 2s. Another time he 'bought five fowls at the door' for 5s.

An innkeeper's bill for a party of 11 people in 1853 gives us some notion of other costs. This was the *Buller's Arms Inn* in Sidwell Street. Suppers were charged at 1s. a head, breakfast at 1s., luncheons at 6d., dinners at 1s. 6d. Drink (beer and cider) was additional. Beds for 11 were charged at 7s. 6d. a night for the lot. The total bill for five days' accommodation for 11 people and a horse amounted to £13 12s. 4d.

Or let us look at the prices of ordinary things at the pannier market in Victorian Exeter. In January 1860 butter was selling at 1s. 4d. to 1s. 6d. a pound, eggs at nine or ten for 1s., rabbits at 10d. each. Fowls were 4s. to 6s. a couple. In June, eggs were selling at 16 for 1s., butter at 11d. to 1s. a pound. The autumn brought pheasants for the middle class at 7s. a brace, fowls at 3s. 6d. to 4s. 9d. a couple.

There was little change in these prices by the 'nineties. In the summer of 1890 *St Anne's Well Brewery* offered its Pale Ale at 14d. a gallon, its stout at 18d. Good sound clarets could be had for as little as 12s. a dozen (alas!) and fine old-chateau bottled clarets, 20 years old, were only 100s. a dozen.

There were plenty of houses available for anyone in those golden days, for such they were despite their incidental miseries. The Freehold Land Society, started in the late 'nineties, bought up pieces of suitable land and built working-class houses by the score to let at 2s. 6d. to 4s. 6d. a week. A house at 3s. 6d. a week contained a large kitchen-living room, with scullery at the back and two bedrooms over. For 5s. a week there was a third bedroom in the attic. There was no shortage of houses for sale or to be let in those 'bad old days'.

For the middle class there were plenty of pleasant houses at £18 to £30 a year, say 7s. to 12s. a week. A house in Heavitree, advertised for sale or to be let in 1890, had three bedrooms, a bath, two sitting-rooms, etc., with gardens front and back, all for £18 a year, or to buy at £290. A 'compact detached villa' in Wonford Road, a good neighbourhood, contained four bedrooms, two sitting-rooms, kitchen and offices, and a good garden, to let for £30 a year, or to buy at £450. A large family house in St Leonard's Road (six bedrooms, bathroom, etc., drawing-room, dining-room, kitchen and other offices, extensive servants' quarters in the semi-basement) sold for £525 in 1848 and for £760 in 1904, having been enlarged in the meantime. The same house was let for £55 a year in 1900. In 1950 it sold for £5,000.

In the summer of 1914, the last golden summer of civilisation, most people in Exeter were as well off as they have ever been. Only in the West Quarter was there still great poverty and a multitude of ragged children. At Exeter market in early June, eggs were 13 for 1s., butter 1s. a pound, potatoes 1s. 2d. a score, onions 1d. a pound, and foreign tomatoes 6d. a pound. Peas were 1s. 6d. a peck, gooseberries 3d. a pound, but the season was early as yet. Rabbits were 6d. to 9d. each, and chickens for the middle class were 6s. or 7s. a couple.

The newly married could buy 'a useful satin walnut suite' for £5 15s., and Axminster carpet at 5s. 9d. a yard. The best Wilton was 6s. 6d. a yard. And you could go on a half-day trip to London on the old London & South Western Railway for 6s. 6d.

Victorian Fortunes

Exeter had ceased to be an industrial or commercial city by the early 19th century, so there were no large industrial fortunes to be made during the Victorian period. The largest fortunes came from banking, and there somewhere round about £100,000 to £130,000 was the maximum figure. To obtain the equivalent value today (1960) in purchasing power we have to multiply by about five for the period 1860-1914. Thus the rich bankers of Exeter left the equivalent of half a million or rather more; and even this takes no account of the severity of modern taxation and of death duties. Before 1894, when Death Duties were first introduced, a fortune passed on almost unimpaired and the next generation, if it had any sense, was able to add to it appreciably. The most potent factor in piling up a large Victorian fortune was having a rich father; but there were also a few self-made men like Henry Willey, the gas engineer, and T.M. Kingdon, the upholsterer, and others.

Samuel Barnes, the noted Exeter surgeon who died in December 1858, left nearly £45,000 (worth a good £200,000 by 1960). His only son, William Barnes, became a partner in Sanders & Co. (generally known as the Exeter Bank), and left the substantial sum of £100,958 at his death in 1892. He lived in state at Great Duryard, his father's house before him.

The senior partner of the Exeter Bank was Edward Andrew Sanders, of Stoke House, the third generation of the family to run the bank. He had inherited a substantial fortune from his father in 1839 and when he died in 1905, at the age of 82, he left £129,797.

Other banking families were the Snows, the Nations, and the Milfords. The Snows were the senior partners in the City Bank (though not among the original founders in 1786) and lived at Franklyn House in St Thomas. Thomas Snow, wine merchant and banker, died in 1875 leaving nearly £90,000. His eldest son, also the senior partner in the City Bank at this time, moved to Cleve House above Exwick, where he died in January 1899 leaving a fortune of £118,026. A third generation followed in the City Bank, which was eventually absorbed by the National Provincial Bank in 1918.

The City Bank had been founded by the Milfords, Nations, and Clarkes, Samuel Milford being a founder-partner. In the mid-Victorian decades Frederick Milford lived at Matford House (once a Barnes residence) and there he died leaving, however, less than £21,000. John Milford, probably his father, lived at Coaver on the Topsham Road, where he died in April 1888 at the great age of 96 leaving a fortune of £57,209.

William Nation (1790-1861) was of the third generation of bankers, but may have retired from active banking at the time of his death. He, too, had inherited a considerable fortune from his father. When he died in 1861 at 25 Southernhay Place, he left about £120,000. His son, William Hamilton Codrington Nation (1843-1914) was better known as a minor Victorian dramatist and died in a Dover hotel leaving well over £300,000.

The bankers were the richest people in Victorian Exeter and their large and opulent houses ringed the city—Stoke House, Great Duryard, Cleve, Matford, Coaver, and Franklyn.

Among other well-to-do men of this generation was Mark Kennaway the solicitor, who had a finger in many pies, and died in 1875 worth nearly £50,000. A curious character was Kent Kingdon, who lived for many years at Taddyforde House on the Cowley Road. He and his father had had a prosperous upholsterer's business in Fore Street. At the time of his death in 1889 he was described as 'retired cabinet maker'. He left a fortune of just under £50,000 which one must assume was mainly the result of a good deal of judicious investment in property.

Successful professional and business men of the first generation might reckon to leave about £20,000 or so in Victorian days. Edward Ashworth, the well known architect and church restorer, left £18,765 in 1896. Segar Bastard, a retired hop merchant, left £18,348 in 1902. Henry Willey, the gas engineer, left £20,877 in 1894.

The Thornton Wests, who built Streatham Hall in 1867, were by far the richest family in Exeter in the latter half of the 19th century, but theirs was not Exeter money. It came from a vast merchant and ship-owning business in London. Richard Thornton West died in 1878 leaving £1 million in personal estate. His eldest son died in 1900 leaving some £440,000, and his widow died in 1902 leaving over £430,000. This rich family, who had chosen Exeter for their residence and built a mansion here, tragically died out within 35 years and made very little impact on the city. Nevertheless, they left behind three tangible memorials—St David's church, Streatham Hall (now known as Reed Hall), and the County Cricket Ground.

Entertainment in Former Days

For the great majority of the people of Exeter, entertainment was a very different affair in the early years of this century from what it is today. Radio and television were far in the future. The motor car had been invented but very few people actually owned a car or even had ever ridden in one. The cinema was known but there was no permanent cinema in Exeter until the year 1911.

If we look at a local newspaper for the year 1908, we can see how most people amused themselves. There was, of course, the Theatre Royal which had stood at the top of Langbrook Street since 1887, when its predecessor had been burnt to the ground in the most disastrous fire in the history of English theatres. The Victoria Hall in Queen Street showed films during the summer and held dances in the winter. The Hippodrome opened in November 1908, on the site of the old Subscription Rooms. This was an enterprise financed by the well-known comedian Fred Karno.

The pleasures of those days seem very unsophisticated to us, but gave tremendous enjoyment. There was, for example, the Exeter Cart-Horse Parade on Whit Monday. Judging took place at the Higher Barracks early in the morning, followed by a grand procession of the decorated cart-horses with bands playing through the streets from half-past ten until half-past twelve. The prizes were then distributed in Bedford Circus, everyone went home for dinner and there were sports in the afternoon. The whole city was decorated with flags for this colourful event, citizens being especially asked to make a good display. The Cart-Horse Parade lapsed during the Great War and was never resumed. Another simple pleasure had gone for good.

For those who did not wish to spend the day in Exeter, there were excursions on the *Duke* or *Duchess of Devonshire* from Exmouth. The Exmouth Line was a vastly profitable one to the railway company, and new halts were opened at Polsloe Bridge and Clyst St Mary and Digby in the summer of 1908. A day trip to Exmouth cost 1s. return. It was possible to go to Bournemouth on a Bank Holiday trip for 4s. and to Portsmouth or Padstow for 4s. 6d. For those who stayed at home there were musical Afternoon Teas at the Central Café where one could have tea and unlimited music for 6d.

Films reached Exeter at the beginning of this century. No one has yet discovered when the first moving pictures were shown in the city. At the Victoria Hall there were seasonal visits of West's Animated Pictures. At these there was one of the earliest attempts at talkies, the sound being provided by a gramophone placed near the projector, but the results were erratic. Apart from these seasonal visits the first cinemas in Exeter were converted shops. The very first one was the Empire Electric Theatre which stood in High Street opposite Bedford Street. This opened in July 1911, and offered a continuous performance from 3 until 10.30 p.m. with the bait 'Come when you like, leave when you like'. This was an enormous

71   The Theatre Royal.

attraction. The seats were soft, unlike anything hitherto known, and children could see the show around two or three times for 2d. or 3d. Adults paid 3d., 6d., or 1s. Music was provided by a woman pianist immediately beneath the screen in an atmosphere thick with cigarette smoke. She played continuously for hours on end, watching the distorted picture, and trying to ensure harmony between her music and the scene above her head.

The second cinema was the City Palace which opened in Fore Street in a former grocer's shop before the end of 1911. In 1912 came the Queen's Hall in Paris Street, later renamed the Palladium. The Queen's Hall opened in September and the King's Hall, in Okehampton Street, opened in early October. The fifth and last cinema was the Franklin behind the restaurant of that name in Fore Street. This provided Saturday afternoon entertainment for hundreds of uproarious children for 1d. per head. The films that were shown in 1912 have titles that seem quite characteristic of those innocent days, titles such as 'For the Honour of the Family', 'The Soul of a Violin', 'Foiled by a Girl', 'The Empty Cot'. It is easy to smile at these old titles, just as it is to laugh at the idiotic fashions of the past, but our tastes will seem just as odd (and perhaps not so pleasant) to those who follow us in a hundred years' time.

It was possible in those days to have an evening out with one's wife or girl friend for a total cost of 1s. 6½d. Two seats at the music hall or theatre cost 1s. (1s. 6d. if one was trying to make an impression), a packet of cigarettes 2d., a glass of beer 1½d., and a glass of port for the lady 3d. If supper followed the evening entertainment, then a plate of sausage and mash cost 4d. and a really expensive meal was steak and chips at 1s. 6d.

The Coming of the Motor-Car

In the year 1960 some 15,000 motor vehicles were registered in Exeter alone. Besides these, tens of thousands registered in the county habitually used the city roads and streets. In the summer holidays these were added to by the tens of thousands that poured in from all parts of Britain: but even in normal weeks it was clear that the motor-car was one of the most conspicuous and intractable of all the problems that faced the city. If only it had never been invented! Or if invented, then never allowed to run in this small and crowded country. But no one could foresee sixty years earlier this appalling maelstrom of vehicles, nor the perpetual slaughter and mutilation, and the perpetual poisonous smell in the streets. In those days it was hardly more than an exciting new toy.

The very first car to enter Exeter was a Benz, shown in a circus in Pinhoe Road in 1897 as a special attraction. Early in 1898 came the first car to drive into Exeter, a Daimler driven (and pushed) by Mr Sturmey from Land's End to John o' Groats. Mr Sturmey stayed at Pople's *New London Hotel* where his car attracted the attention of Mr William Shepherd, and his son, local engineers and owners of the Albion Works in Longbrook Terrace. By September 1899 they had designed and manufactured their own car and it was on the road. Mr Reid, a jeweller, built the second car, a copy of a Benz, which was on the road early in 1900. This car would carry four adults around Exeter at an average speed of 12 miles an hour on the level, and six miles an hour up not too steep a hill.

When the registration of cars was made compulsory on 1 January 1904, there were 12 proud owners of private cars in the city. The first registration letters for Exeter were FJ, being the initials of the then mayor, Mr F.J. Widgery, and FJ1 was owned by Mr J.E. Norman, of Norman & Pring, the brewers. His was a seven-horse-power Benz; but FJ2, owned by Mr A.J. Brooking, the pawnbroker, was registered as a 'Steam Car Locomobile' of four-and-a-half-horse-power, dog-cart type. FJ3 belonged to Mr Budd, the surgeon whose daughter—Miss Katherine Rose Budd—deserves record as the first woman driver to take out a licence in Exeter (25 February 1904). She did not renew her licence in the following year.

Other early owners of cars (by January 1904) included A.H. Wheaton, H.A. Willey, Charles Ross (the tailor), P.V.H. Hoare, and Hodges the engineers. The number of cars increased very slowly indeed, the 13th car not being registered until the end of July 1905. By the end of 1907 there were 70 private cars registered in Exeter; by the beginning of 1912 there were 225.

Early in the year 1902, H.A. Willey, who has already been referred to as a live wire in Exeter, brought down from Coventry 'the well-known motor-car expert', Mr Sturmey, to discuss with the Chamber of Commerce the establishment of a motor-car industry in the city. Nothing came of this meeting (thank God, for what sort of city would we have had now?), but in the local directory for 1902 William Shepherd and Son styled themselves 'motor-car manufacturers' among other things.

In 1914 most of the streets were peaceful and empty of traffic. In that year only 577 driving licences were issued. But the Great War of 1914-18

72 Removal of the wooden pontoon bridge before the opening of the new iron Exe bridge in 1905.

gave a tremendous impetus to the development of motor-vehicles, and even in a rather remote and non-industrial city like Exeter the number of licences issued jumped to over 1,300 in 1920. The scourge had begun; the flood-gates were breaking down.

Victorian Exeter lasted on until the year 1914, though the Queen had died 13 years earlier. The flashy, vulgar age of Edward VII made no impression on respectable cathedral cities like Exeter, or indeed anywhere much in provincial England. It was the year 1914 that marked the end of the Victorian Age for most people in England.

During that time Exeter had grown very slowly. For centuries she had been one of the leading cities of England, usually fourth or fifth in size; but during the 18th century the industrial and commercial towns of the Midlands and the North had shot ahead. Their industries were expanding; Exeter's were disappearing, certainly by 1820. By 1800 Exeter had dropped to 14th in size among provincial towns; by 1860, fortieth. A large boundary extension in 1913 brought the population to 60,000; but Exeter was still a rather quiet cathedral city, largely residential, with some small local industries tucked away near the river for the most part, with good shops that served a wide area of the county also, bustling on market-days, with narrow crowded streets down which the electric trams groaned and squealed slowly, while the horse-cabs waited patiently here and there in quiet backwaters; and on Sundays the church bells everywhere over the city roof-tops and old ladies setting forth in all directions clutching prayer-books, with tottering steps and slow.

CHAPTER TEN

Exeter since 1914

THE GREAT WAR OF 1914-18 burst upon a pleasant old cathedral city, but after the first shock life went on pretty much as before. Far in the West of England, Exeter could not be reached by aeroplanes and bombs, and the only privation that the city suffered was the growing shortage of food as the war dragged on and on. People began to wonder if it would ever end. Men disappeared, some never to return to their dear old native city. Wounded soldiers in blue crept around the city streets: one saw them everywhere. Or regiments marched away to the War, with bands playing and mobs of small boys trying to lead the way with home-made flags.

The end of the War came in November 1918 amid rejoicings and tears: at first wild hopes of a new world, then the inevitable disillusion as the politicians got to work. Most of us sooner or later have to pay for our own mistakes: it is only politicians who manage to make other people pay. One cannot learn too soon to have an absolute contempt for them as a class, whatever their creed or the colour of their ties.

But life goes on pleasantly in Exeter whatever lunacy prevails elsewhere, and in 1919 things slowly returned to normal in the city streets. There were many more motor-cars about (but still very few compared with today), and more houses were being built round the outskirts. Even so, you could still get out into the country on foot within fifteen minutes or so from any part of Exeter. Every boy grew up in the 1920s with his own favourite woods to climb in, his favourite little streams for fishing with net and jam-jar, and well known places for picking primroses in the spring and blackberries in the autumn. Our pleasures were simple and our wants were few. Threepence a week pocket money in 1920 offered, if not wealth, at least a variety of interesting possibilities.

High Street in 1919

In the High Street you could still find small shops and family businesses. The directory for the year 1919 speaks almost of another world. At the top of the High Street was The Arcade with the Coffee Tavern on the corner and the Arcade Lecture Hall (whoever used that?). The other end of the Arcade opened into Southernhay West. It was full of interesting little shops, safely out of the rain. A little below the Arcade was the General Post Office (destroyed in 1942). Then came Stanbury (tobacconist) and

73 The Arcade.

Sebley (hosier), followed by Troulan (Optician) and Wynne Tighe (chemists). Next, St John's Hospital School, with Mr Howell as headmaster. Next, Damarell (saddler) and Havills (butchers). Here the narrow Bampfylde Street led in to the beautiful Elizabethan courtyard-house of the Bampfyldes of Poltimore—another victim of 1942. The Bampfyldes had long since ceased to live there and in the years before the Great War the house was occupied by Varwell, Guest & Co. (coal merchants).

On the other corner of Bampfylde Street and High Street stood Depaoli's Café, then came Wilson (fancy draper) followed by the Domestic Bazaar.* This occupied the site of the old *Three Tuns Inn* and had come into existence some time since 1910. Next to the Domestic Bazaar was Joshua Daw (tailor), then the Misses Cornish and King (ladies' outfitters), Freeths (confectioners), the Singer Sewing Machine Co., the Pearl Life Assurance, Randell (boot-maker), then Depree and Young (goldsmiths, etc.) on the corner of Bedford Street.

On the other corner of Bedford Street stood Lloyds Bank, with Deller's Café over it. This corner had been occupied for centuries by the *Half Moon Hotel*, one of the largest hotels in the city, demolished in the summer of 1912. In former times it had been much frequented by the leading tradesmen in the High Street, especially those of St Stephen's parish. They used to meet regularly here after dinner to enjoy their glass of grog and smoke Dutch cut tobacco in long clay pipes, returning to their shops about

* There was no Woolworths in Exeter in 1919 but Marks and Spencer had opened the Penny Bazaar near the top of Queen Street (No. 5) in 1912. In 1918 they opened a second bazaar at No. 259 High Street, a small emporium on part of the site where they traded from 1951 to 1982. Woolworths did not come to Exeter until 1924. The coming of these chain-stores, and especially their recent developments, is an important piece of social history. It brought changes in shopping habits and, after the war of 1939-45, marked changes in social habits.

74 Corner of High Street and Bedford Street in the summer of 1908. The *Half Moon* hotel was demolished in 1912.

four o'clock to receive their London letters. This would be in the early 19th century, before the railway had reached Exeter. At the annual beating of the parish boundary of St Stephen's, the parishioners dined at the *Half Moon*. Generally, thirty or forty sat around the festive board and the occasion was considered the most convivial gathering in the city. Doubtless it was one of many that made the same claim, for Exonians had the reputation—like all civilised cities—of celebrating any notable occasion with good food, good drink, and cheerful company, regardless of time. It was at the *Half Moon*, on the hotel piano, that Sullivan first played over the music of *The Mikado* to Gilbert.

When the *Half Moon* was demolished, the greater part of the site was taken over by Deller's Café, the principal entrance to which was in Bedford Street. Dellers, as it was known to all citizens and to holiday-makers all over England, was built in a remarkable baroque, even rococo, style. There was nothing else quite like it anywhere. Wherever one sat, on any floor, its plan enabled one to see all who entered and left. It opened its doors in December 1916 and became a meeting-place for the younger generation of Exeter, and so it remained until it was destroyed in the air-raid of May 1942. The destruction of Dellers, with all its happy associations for so many people (how many courtships must have blossomed within its walls and alcoves!), was perhaps the greatest single loss to Exeter in all the destruction of that terrible night. In its brief life of barely twenty-five years, it had

75 Deller's Café interior: a popular café, with galleries and a light orchestra.

become part of the social history of the city: its disappearance has made Exeter a duller place altogether for the younger generation.

Returning to the High Street, Green & Son (drapers) followed next after Lloyds Bank. They occupied the site of the famous *New Inn*. This, despite its name, was actually the oldest inn in Exeter, having been built by the dean and chapter of the cathedral, the ground landlords, about the year 1445. It remained the principal inn of the city until the removal of the Cloth Fair from its premises to St John's Hospital in 1778, and its decline was probably accelerated by the building of the *New London Inn* 16 years later. The famous Apollo Room of this inn, with its superbly decorated plaster ceiling (made in 1680-90) could still be seen by the ladies who shopped in Green's after the Great War.

Next to Green's was St Stephen's Church, then came the offices of the *Western Evening Herald* and the *Western Daily Mercury*, followed by Shapley (confectioner), Chamberlain (stationer), Frost (hairdresser), Cann (tailors), and then Colsons (drapers) who still occupied the site occupied by Colson & Spark as far back as 1828, and probably back to 1792 when the business started as linen drapers. Colsons is now Dingles.

Below Colsons were Rush (florists), Palmer & Edwards (bakers and confectioners), and then the London Joint City and Midland Bank (now HSBC) on the corner of Martins Lane. On the other corner stood Hoskins & Son (bakers and restaurant), a property which was still held as a copyhold of

King's College, Cambridge, the last piece of college copyhold to fall in. It had originally been given to St James' Priory, founded in 1141 near the river, by Baldwin de Redvers, earl of Devon. The priory was suppressed by Henry VI as an alien house (it was dependent on the French abbey of St Martin des Champs in Paris) and its properties given to King's College in 1444.

Next to this property stood Gould & Allen (grocers), another old Exeter business. William Gould, grocer, had started here in 1803 and the firm was still here at the end of the Second World War. Next door was Hinton Lake (chemists); then came Browns (florists), Lakes (gold and silver smiths), Brooking (electrical engineers), Fox (hosier), Stocker (tailors), Lemmon (chemist), Shapley (confectioner), Wykes (photographer), Bright (tailors), Peters & Hamlin (wholesale grocers), Webbers (ironmongers), Trelease (hosier, etc.), Boots (chemists), Veitch (seedsman, etc.), Wippells (church furnishers), Fox, Fowlers Bank, National Provincial Bank, Maypole Dairy, Tannar (boot and shoe makers), Timothy White (chemists), and then Broadgate. Between Broadgate and the top of South Street were the National Provincial Bank, then St Petrock's Church; followed by Morton's boot warehouse, Blacking's Vaults, Richards (hosiers), and Holman, Ham (chemists) on the corner.

Crossing the High Street to the North Street corner, and returning along the other side, we would have started in 1919 with Hepworths (outfitters), then Johnsons (dyers), and so on. There is no space to deal with this side of the street in detail, but it presented the same picture of mostly family businesses, some of them of long standing. Among these latter were Wippell Bros. and Row (ironmongers at Nos. 243-4) and Tucker & Glenn (bootmakers at No. 255). Both were in their third generation. By 1960 the street contained little but national banks and insurance companies, chain stores and multiple shops. There is hardly a family business left in the main street. This change, due mainly to rising rents and rates, was operating before the Second World War; and the enormous inflation of site values and of local rates after 1945 completed the process. By 1960 the old names could be counted on the fingers of one hand.

Between the Wars

Exeter had grown very slowly since the end of the first World War, when it had just over 60,000 people. By 1960 it still had fewer than 80,000 and it had not changed its essential character over the previous forty years. In the census of 1931 there were 66,029 people. Out of every hundred people in the city, 45 were gainfully occupied, 21 were at school or college, 31 were not gainfully occupied (mostly housewives), and three had retired from some gainful occupation.

Out of every hundred occupied persons in the city, only 30 were engaged in manufacturing or producing things; 40 were engaged in buying and selling and distributing; 26 were engaged in supplying various personal services, and three in administration of some kind or another. So 70 people in every hundred who were employed were engaged in providing services in the widest sense of the word, and that was the essential character of Exeter. Because of this, too, wages tended to be low. In August 1939 craftsmen in the building trades were getting 1s. 7d. an hour for a 44-hour week. This produced an average weekly wage of 69s. 8d. (in 1960 it was £9 5s. 2d.). Labourers in the building trade got 1s. 2¼d. an hour, or 52s. 3d. a week. Now (1960) they average about £8 a week or slightly more. In the engineering trades, fitters, turners, and smiths worked a 47-hour week for a wage of 65s. So, generally speaking, a typical labouring income in pre-war Exeter was a little over 50s. a week, while a craftsman's wage was round about 70s. Top men in highly skilled trades, such as printing, could get around about £4 a week, but such men were relatively few.

During the 1930s one of the principal changes in the appearance of the city was the systematic attack on the slums of the West Quarter. The worst of these were demolished—unfortunately without any kind of record of what was destroyed, because it was in fact one of the most interesting parts of Exeter from the standpoint of social history, full of decayed merchants' houses and other relics of the past. The former slum dwellers were rehoused partly in the old area, but mainly on new estates on the outskirts of the city, so that the city began to lose its ancient shape and to spread out into the surrounding countryside.

Another great change of these years was the replacement of the old electric trams by buses. The last tram ran on 19 August 1931 and was driven by the same city worthy who had driven the first tram in 1905.

Apart from such changes as these, life went on in Exeter much as usual, and it was to this quiet city that the Second World War came in September 1939.

The Burning of the City

In the museum and art gallery of the beautiful South German city of Würzburg there is a modern painting called 'The Night of the Burning'. It shows the whole of that city in flames, set on fire by the Royal Air Force in late March 1945, a completely unnecessary and wanton act of destruction. In the space of a few hours the monuments of more than a thousand years perished. Würzburg was a city very like Exeter, only even more beautiful. It had no military or industrial importance. It had a cathedral, a university, a score of fine churches, hospitals and almshouses, a magnificent castle, many beautiful streets. To anyone coming from Exeter that painting strikes home, for it might well have been our city in the year 1942. There could not be a more powerful illustration of the utter folly of war, of the fact that as any war goes on the barbarians always get the upper hand and the voice of reason and magnanimity is gradually shouted down by those warped beings who have the lust to destroy.

When the Second World War began in September 1939, no one expected that much would happen in Exeter. Nothing had happened in the First World War; but by the summer of 1940 the all-conquering Germans were entrenched only a hundred miles away across the English Channel. Two or three bombs were dropped on the edge of the city one August night in 1940, the first time the people of Exeter had heard a shot fired in anger since the sieges of the Civil War nearly three hundred years earlier. These bombs did little damage, but they were a taste of what was to come.

76 The old City Library, Castle Street.

77 After the air-raid of May 1942: the end of Bedford Circus, one of the most notable pieces of Georgian town-planning in England.

By the spring of 1942 the war in the air had become increasingly savage. The ancient German city of Lübeck was destroyed (probably by mistake) and as a reprisal for this irreparable act of destruction Hitler ordered the destruction of all the most beautiful and historic cities in England. Almost the first to be chosen for destruction was our own city of Exeter, probably the most disastrous compliment ever paid to a beautiful town. On April 24-25 German aircraft reached the city, dropped bombs, but failed to do much damage. Then in the early morning of 5 May came the main attack. Under a full moon about thirty German aircraft flew up the shining estuary about midnight, and for an hour and a half rained fire-bombs down upon the old city. Within a few minutes it seemed as though it was on fire from end to end.

Though the spectacle was terrifying, the number of casualties was remarkably small. Altogether 80 people were killed, and rather more than a hundred injured. But the material destruction was very great. Some 38 acres of the built-up area suffered complete destruction or serious damage. Three-quarters of the principal shopping area was destroyed, together with a large number of houses, workshops, and warehouses. Six churches were either destroyed or severely damaged. Of these, the greatest loss was the little medieval church of St Lawrence which stood in the High Street; and the Cathedral itself suffered severe damage on the south side. Of the 20,000 houses in the city, 1,500 were wholly destroyed, 2,700 were seriously damaged, and a great number of others damaged to some degree. Among the public buildings that were lost were the fine Lower Market, much of the old City Hospital on Heavitree Road, and Dellers Café. The city library was burnt out, losing a tremendous number of books. Fortunately, the city archives, the richest collection in England outside the city of London, had been shifted to a place of safety. The Great Fire was halted at the very doors of the muniment room, as one can still see to this day. The Germans claimed that they had dropped a thousand bombs upon the city that night; and the next morning they gloated: 'Exeter was a jewel, and we have destroyed it'.

The Great Fire was a disaster in more senses than one. It was the most savage destruction of the city since the barbaric Danes burnt it, with the abbey, in the year 1003. The war dragged on, the ruins were cleared up as well as possible, but grass grew all over the bombed city, and giant buddleias flourished in broken medieval cellars. We lived through historic times, without perhaps realising it. I saw a gypsy tether his horse beside the ruins of South Street, to feed on the grass-grown ruins, and I saw an old lady picking flowers among the ruins. Many people must have similar recollections of those years. This was history, all around us, with the seagulls wailing above the acres of destruction.

Nearly eight years went by before the work of rebuilding the city was begun. The whole country was impoverished by the long war, the material damage in scores of towns was enormous, and it was only with the greatest difficulty that the most elementary repairs could be carried out. Savage though the burning of Exeter was, it was little compared with the blind havoc wreaked upon some of the most beautiful cities of Europe later in the war, notably the utter wrecking of Würzburg and Dresden. For this there was no possible shadow of an excuse. But by this time the savages on both sides, and we had our savages as well as the Germans, had got the upper hand. And all the time Exeter lay in its red and dusty ruins, awaiting the return of peace and reason.

The Silent Revolution

Much in this chapter of the history of Exeter has made rather sad reading for those of us who care for the well-being of the city. But there has been one silent revolution that should not pass unnoticed. It has gone on almost imperceptibly since the early years of this century, yet is none the less dramatic. This is the great saving of human life brought about by the reduction in infant mortality, and that in turn has been achieved by the clearance of the awful slums that still defaced the city within the living memory of many of us, and by the notable advances of medical science and nursing.

78 A street in the West Quarter: Preston Street c.1890.

The earliest reports of the medical officer of health for Exeter show that in the closing years of the 19th century (1896-99) no fewer than 169 children, out of every 1,000 born, died before reaching the age of one year. This was a higher mortality even than London and the great towns generally. Infant mortality was highest among the poorest classes, those who lived in the slums of the West Quarter. We do not know the exact figures for this poverty-stricken area, but in all probability one child in four died here in the first year of life. In York, for example, a city very comparable with Exeter in its social structure and general living conditions, Seebohm Rowntree's enquiry at this same period showed that the infant mortality rate for the city as a whole was 176 per 1,000 births. But the actual rate varied from 94 among 'the servant-keeping class' to 247 in the poorest class. There is no reason to suppose that Exeter would have shown any different figures from this. This was an appalling wastage of human life.

79 Lants Almshouses *c.*1930. Built in 1763 on the city wall in Bartholomew Street, they were removed in 1959 for road-widening.

At Exeter, as in other towns, this high rate had been about halved by 1914, and after the Great War the revolution continued at an increased pace. There were marked fluctuations from year to year, but the trend was always downward. These figures show what was happening:

1896-99	169 deaths per 1,000 births (average for period)
1900	138
1910	97
1920	67
1930	50
1950	32
1950-59	25 (average for the decade)
1960	15

More than five out of six children who would have died in infancy in the closing years of the 19th century are now saved. Or, to put it in another way, many hundreds of people are now walking about Exeter and enjoying life who, fifty or sixty years ago, would have been buried in some forgotten grave.

Whatever social and cultural changes there may have been for the worse in these years, they are outweighed by this saving of human life and by the visible improvement in the standard of living of families who, only a generation ago, lived amid dirt, rags, and ill-health. There is still much to do. Though many new born infants are now saved, the post-neo-natal mortality is still too high. The gap between the social classes, so marked in the late 19th century, still shows no signs of narrowing in this respect even in the 1960s. Nor has poverty been abolished. It has changed its character to a large extent. It has become less visible, among the very old, whereas formerly it was all too visible among the ragged children whom one rarely sees nowadays. There is much to do before we can relapse into complacency in Exeter.

Exeter in 1960

Eighteen years and more have gone by since the city was devastated. Much has been rebuilt in a commonplace style that might belong anywhere: it is not distinctive as the old Exeter was, with its rich regional flavour. Once more Exeter is the capital of South-Western England, and its shops and streets are as crowded as they ever were. It is still the same kind of city, with seven out of ten of its occupied population providing services of one kind or another. In numbers it grows very slowly, but with the clearing of the congested areas it spreads more and more into the surrounding country. Yet green fields are still visible from most of its streets even today, and it remains one of the most attractive cities in England to look at and to live in.

   Its two greatest enemies are the motor-car and the speculative builder. In 1947 there were rather fewer than four thousand private cars registered in the city. Now there are more than twice as many, and more than twice

80   Paul Street Car Park.

81 Commentary from 1959 by Frederick Beamiss.

82 Nos. 74 and 76 East Wonford Hill. These early 18th-century houses were demolished in 1966 for a road scheme.

as many commercial vehicles. The narrow streets are being torn apart and much of old Exeter is being lost because everything must be sacrificed to enable the motorist to go one mile an hour faster or to save his withered legs from a moment's walking. The motorist's demands upon our city are endlessly greedy and selfish. But people are more important than vehicles. The motorist must be kept firmly in his place, for he brings the kiss of death wherever he goes.

As for the speculative builder, he seizes daily upon the large houses that were built in late Georgian and early Victorian days, in their large, well-tree'd gardens, and clears the whole site in order to make the maximum profit. The old house comes down, and the beautiful trees, inherited from our grandfathers and great-grandfathers, are sacrificed in order to cram two or three more tatty little houses into the old garden. In twenty years' time, the opulent and seemly houses that were built in an age of elegance will have been replaced by a desert of bricks and concrete.

There is another profound difference between the city of 1960 and that of a hundred years ago. A century ago, two centuries ago, Exeter was a cultured place, the social and intellectual capital of a rich and varied province. Look how highly Richard Ford spoke of it in the 1830s, when he came to live here! Today the city library, burnt out nearly twenty years

83 Devon and Exeter Institution and Law Library in the evening.

ago, is still a shambles. The failure to rebuild it is the greatest disgrace in the post-war history of the city. It is clear that books are not considered to be important in modern Exeter. How vastly different from our Victorian forefathers when they founded the Free Library in 1869!

This failure to provide a good library for the people of Exeter is only the most obvious symptom of some obscure disease that goes very deep. Somewhere between 1860 and now, Exeter ceased to be a cultured city. It would be instructive to trace exactly when and how this profound rot set in, a fascinating and melancholy problem for some social historian. I suspect that the rot was going on rapidly during the later years of the 19th century: but what brought it about? Were late Victorians so different from their fathers and grandfathers? Why did the learned societies of Exeter disappear one by one? Why does the Devon and Exeter Institution, that learned library which Richard Ford so greatly admired, gather dust silently, and struggle to make ends meet? The people of Exeter seem to be able to exist happily without any good music: the theatre, centuries old as a tradition in the city, staggers from crisis to crisis.* We cannot blame the cinema or television: the rot had set in long before either made its appearance. George Gissing noted in the early 1890s that Exeter people did not support good music even then. In a letter to his sister (30 December 1892), written from No. 1, St Leonard's Terrace, where he was living, he says: 'We went to hear the *Elijah*, but it was very poorly done. Curious that the people of Exeter will not support anything good in drama or music.'

---

* On 29 September 1962 it closed its doors for the last time, so ending the continuous history of the theatre in Exeter since 1737—a period of 225 years. Plays had occasionally been performed at the old *Seven Stars Hotel*, which stood at the St Thomas end of the Exe Bridge (some of us can just remember it) but in 1737 the first real theatre building was erected in Waterbeer Street, just where the police station stood until very recent years. For the history of the various theatres in Exeter, several of which perished in great fires, see E.R. Delderfield's *Cavalcade by Candlelight* (published at Exmouth; 1950).

In another letter he complains of Exeter that 'intellectually it is very dull'. This could never have been said forty years earlier.

For the last two generations or more Exeter has ceased to care about any of these things. It has changed greatly for the worse in this respect. The new university, established in 1956 after its abortive start so many centuries ago, cannot fail in time to bring the ancient culture of Exeter back to life. Two or three generations are after all a very short time. Caerwysc, Isca, Exancester, Exeter—more than seventy generations of people have opened their eyes and closed them for the last time in this ancient city of ours.

And there remains much that is beautiful to look at. There are still dark ilex trees overhanging old stone walls, and there are the little sandstone churches up and down the main streets, with their startling red towers against the blue-and-white sky. And though the river-front has been despoiled in part, there is still the long deserted quay with its noble warehouses, built just before the coming of the railways; and the canal, probably the most beautiful ship-canal in England, carrying very little traffic but providing the most peaceful of walks along its banks down to Topsham and beyond, to where the Exe scents the open sea: the same shining river that brought the pre-historic ships up to earliest Exeter more than two thousand years ago.

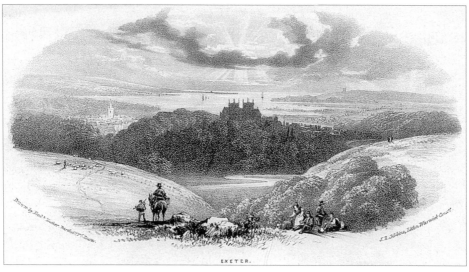

84 Lithograph by J.R. Jobbins after J. Tucker *c*.1825.

CHAPTER ELEVEN

Exeter since 1960

by Hazel Harvey

Exeter has seen huge changes since 1960. As mentioned above, the expansion of the built-up area had begun with slum-clearance in 1929, the Burnthouse Lane estate rehousing the inhabitants of Paul Street and the West Quarter. The spread had continued in the 1950s, when accommodation lost in the 1942 Blitz was replaced in airy council estates on the slopes of Stoke Hill and the fields of Whipton. In the 1960s and '70s the green hillsides above St Thomas and Exwick were covered with streets of little brick houses and flats. Industrial estates sprawled over farmland at Sowton, Matford and Marsh Barton. Large offices moved from the city centre to the outskirts. The local newspaper, which had once had its office on the High Street, and later on Sidwell Street, moved its journalists and printing presses to the Sowton Industrial Estate. The Royal Devon and Exeter Hospital had found its accommodation increasingly cramped on Southernhay. It moved to a concrete tower at Wonford, but this succumbed to concrete cancer after only 25 years and had to be replaced. The new low-rise hospital consists of long corridors with many wings. It has also taken in the Orthopaedic Hospital and the West of England Eye Infirmary, which had been independent. The Meteorological Office moved from Bracknell in 2003 into purpose-built accommodation on the edge of town.

No longer are homes, workplaces, shops and amenities within walking distance of each other. Colin Hewitt, a member of the Devon branch of Transport 2000, has summarised the effects:

'Hoskins had outspoken views on the impact of road traffic. Perhaps it was fitting that, like his two brothers and an Exonian cousin, he never drove a car. His castigation of the road establishment and their idea of progress was summed up in a final flourish in his last TV appearance. Describing the fate of Exeter after the ravages of the Luftwaffe, he said, "... they did terrible damage, but since then the City Council to my mind has nearly finished the job off". These uncompromising sentiments are borne out by the evidence of various development plans produced by the City Council in the dark ages before the 1974 reorganisation

85 Marsh Barton Industrial Estate 2003.

86 Royal Devon and Exeter Hospital in March 1996 just before the demolition of the 1971 tower block.

transferred the responsibilities for transport to Devon County Council. Western Way would have floated on an overpass across Bull Meadow. Hoskins was particularly gratified that he and his fellow campaigners won a reprieve for this park. The rest of the inner bypass went ahead, including the gyratory system of the new twin Exe Bridges—the City Council's last hoorah in its attempts to solve the problems of traffic congestion. Hoskins did have the satisfaction of initiating the high-profile operation for The House That Moved—removing it from the route of the new Western Way.

'The problem of congestion stubbornly refuses to be resolved. The 1960s witnessed the first surge in car ownership, which continues inexorably. The 2001 census shows that over 40,000 cars were registered in the city. 72.4 per cent of households have one or more cars. Car usage is higher in the UK than in the EU. To try to reduce it has

87 The House That Moved in transit in 1961, being winched up to West Street.

88 Paul Street, junction with Goldsmith Street. These houses and shops were replaced with the massive blank wall of the Guildhall Shopping Centre.

become a major objective of national and local government. A whole raft of schemes have been introduced: Park and Ride, Kiss and Ride (wife drives you to the station), Traffic Management and Calming, pedestrian zones, bus lanes, cycle paths, car-sharing, and improvements to public transport. "Sustainability" is the current watchword, one that would have pleased Hoskins enormously. "Not before time", we can hear him say. On the other hand, we may be sure that the proposed redevelopment of Princesshay and Bedford Street would not have endeared itself to him, with its increase in city-centre parking. 20,000 Exonians have signed a petition against this development, collected by a group called Exeter People's Choice. Pedestrians do have one useful new amenity with the recent opening of the elegant footbridge ('Miller's Crossing') linking Exwick Fields with the city centre at Blackaller Weir.

'Hoskins deplored the loss of many Devonshire railway branch-lines in the infamous Beeching era of the mid- to late 1960s, especially as he had made extensive use of these local services when visiting every parish in Devon while preparing his *magnum opus* on the county. However, the axe was not so brutal for Exeter itself. Five flourishing lines still serve the city and its hinterland. This keeps many cars out of the city altogether.

'A better use of buses has also helped, and will help, to reduce traffic levels. However, the city council's short-sighted decision in 1969 to sell its bus operations to Devon General was a retrograde step. Since then, the County Transport Policies and Programmes have made

89 Demolishing the city wall for Western Way.

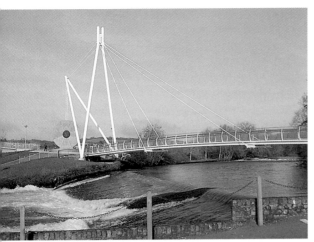

90 Miller's Crossing foot and cycle bridge, opened in November 2002. The design incorporated two giant millstones.

91 Aerial view taken in 2003 shows Western Way serving the twin Exe Bridges of 1969 and 1972.

an impact. The city-wide minibus service in the '80s and '90s (the first such scheme in the UK) showed what imagination and commitment can achieve. Unfortunately, the bus station was moved to Paris Street in 1964, from Paul Street, where it had been conveniently close to Exeter Central railway station.

'Buses have enjoyed privileged access to the High Street, barred to other traffic since it was pedestrianised in 1975. (Critics describe it as a "linear bus station". Countless minibuses stand with engines running.) Hoskins had bitterly opposed the city council's development plans in the 1960s which would have involved pushing the High Street dual carriageway through to Queen Street, at the expense of the splendid Tudor frontages opposite Dingle's.

'Increased car ownership has brought with it a major shift in the pattern of retailing. The resulting out-of-town developments have themselves contributed to the increasing ownership and use of cars. Food retailing began this change in the early 1970s and has been followed by the growth in non-food retailing after the planning permission for CRS Homeworld on the Sowton estate in the 1980s. The zoning of residential and commercial areas has created a situation in which access to cars has become a necessity and thus a major challenge to the planners.

'The arrival of the M5 on Exeter's doorstep in the late 1970s, followed by the upgrading of the A30 (the A38 to Plymouth had already been constructed earlier in the decade), and the new North Devon Link, have made Exeter even more of a regional centre. British Rail's response came in the form of the "125" High-Speed Trains to London and the North, as well as improved track, trains and services on the Waterloo line, which itself proved to be a convenient link into Eurostar services to the continent. Railway privatisation in the mid-'90s was not the panacea that its proponents had promised, the First Great Western operator being only a very pale shadow of its illustrious forebears. We can be certain that Hoskins would have added his share of obloquy in condemning the whole ill-conceived shambles.

'Exeter Airport literally "took off" in the last quarter of the century. In addition to a growth of flights internally and Europe-wide, the package-

92 The High Street in the mid-1960s when the dual carriageway was still open to cars and double-decker buses.

93 High Street in 2004.

holiday industry also forged ahead, bringing it the status of an international airport.

'Finally, the canal. After an ignominious period when its only commercial users were the sludge boats from the Countess Wear Sewage Works, it now, like most other waterways in Britain, accommodates a flourishing leisure trade, running pleasure boats to the Double Locks and Turf taverns. Hoskins would probably have welcomed this happy development.'

The foregoing paragraphs have touched on campaigns against the City Council's policies in the 1960s. At that time several architects and other educated citizens were unhappy about the threats to historic buildings which had survived the Blitz. The Higher Market faced demolition to facilitate development of 'The Golden Heart'. Bedford Circus and Higher Summerlands had been bulldozed rather than repaired. There was even a danger that Southernhay West might be demolished, as its Georgian houses, designed for domestic use, were not easy to adapt for offices. The Junior Chamber of Commerce was calling for car parking on the lawns of Southernhay.

The Civic Trust had recently been set up nationally 'to promote a pride of place'. An Exeter Group was formed, including the architect John Radford, the archaeologist Aileen Fox, Bishop Wilfrid Westall, Dr Fortescue-Foulkes, the historian Robert Newton, and the head of St Luke's Training College, James Smeall. Exeter Civic Society was launched and Hoskins was invited to become its first Chairman. Lady Fox took over from him in 1967. She remembers, 'From the start it was emphasised that we were not a preservation society but were interested in the all-round and balanced development of the city.' The new society campaigned vigorously and successfully to retain the Higher Market, to see the blitzed City Library replaced, to preserve the western skyline and to lay out a riverside walk. They also called for a local history museum. This was established in Rougemont House but now has splendid galleries in the Royal Albert Memorial Museum.

The Civic Society's team of vigilantes monitored planning applications for each area. They made surveys of possible conservation areas and the City Council took these on board. They argued against housing development in the Duryard Valley, saying that it should be kept as a Valley Park. The Council has since embraced this concept and developed green wedges all around the city.

One of the Valley Parks runs alongside the river. It was created as part of extensive flood prevention works. Low-lying St Thomas had suffered from repeated inundations since records began. In October and December 1960 swirling torrents flooded Exwick fields and a thousand shops and homes in the main streets of St Thomas. A £4,000,000 flood defence scheme took from 1965 to 1977 to complete. Stretching seven miles from Cowley Bridge to Countess Wear, it involved digging a flood relief channel, designing new twin Exe Bridges which would allow the water to pass underneath more freely, and building promenades along the banks, so fulfilling one of the wishes listed by the new Civic Society in 1961.

94 Exeter's Public Library (1965) designed by the City Council's architect H.B. Rowe, with picture windows looking onto Rougemont Gardens.

95 Built-up skyline in Exwick and flood relief works.

Hoskins described the post-industrial Quay in 1960 as 'deserted'. Forty years later the Electricity Generating Station is empty, the gas holders are no longer used, Willey's foundries have closed down. Shilhay, too, has been cleared of its small industries and has been used for an award-winning housing development. Exeter's important wool industry is remembered in the names of its courts: Carders, Fullers, Weavers, Dyers, Teazle and so on. In 1982 all the small businesses in the Quay Cellars were moved to Marsh Barton.

Year upon year since this clearance the Council has debated the best use of the quayside and the canal basin. They have set up architectural competitions and public consultations. The Custom House has stood empty since the VAT officers moved to Exeter Airport in 1989 and the other clerks were found more economical space in Renslade House. The 19th-century warehouses on the Quay were converted to prestigious office accommodation by inserting a glass atrium for a lift between the two stone blocks. This is attractive, but it means that the Quay can no longer

96 Renslade House, New Bridge Street and old Exebridge.

97 Renslade House and Exebridge North.

be used for filming costume drama, as it was for the television series of *The Onedin Line.*

There were glory days when the warehouses contained the Exeter Maritime Museum, David Goddard's unique collection of boats from every continent. Some had a story— a rowing boat used to escape from Nazi-occupied Holland, others which had been recovered from attempts to row across the Atlantic single-handed, although the rower had been lost at sea. Some were working boats, rescued at the moment when mass-produced outboard motors and fibre-glass hulls were replacing boats crafted locally from local materials, which had developed their design over centuries for a particular local purpose, pearl-fishing out at sea, perhaps, or nosing up an African river.

The boats filled the warehouses on the Quay; a ride on the ferry across the river was part of the fun, and the Canal Basin held large boats to climb over and explore, including a Danish steam tug and a Chinese junk. Under cover there was a Venetian wedding gondola, with a reed boat from Lake Titicaca, dug-out canoes, catamarans and coracles.

The City Council evicted the Maritime Museum at short notice in 1996, after 27 years, just as it was on the point of applying for lottery funding. The area is now promoted as 'Historic Quayside'. On sunny days it is busy with visitors enjoying the cafes and antiques showrooms or canoeing on the water, but many people still come looking for the Maritime Museum. It was Exeter's major tourist attraction, second only to the cathedral.

Fortunately our beautiful cathedral still stands, providing timeless continuity. It is fully used for services, classical concerts and tours for visitors. On the other hand, the little churches which are such a feature of the city centre have lost their congregations to the peripheries. Five churches have joined to form the Central Parish: Sts Stephen, Pancras, Martin, Olave and Mary Arches. St Petrock's has been converted into a centre where the homeless can get advice, a hot meal and a bath. St Sidwell's has become a community centre, with a café promoting healthy eating, IT tuition, bedsits and a small upstairs chapel.

Hoskins delighted in the continuity of Exeter's history, tracing local place-names through the centuries. This feeling is not shared by today's developers, who are guided by the financial snob-value of a change of name. Exeter's historic Higher Barracks, the best surviving example of a complete cavalry barracks from Napoleonic times, have been developed for housing and dubbed Horseguards. Exminster Hospital is now Devington Park. The address for new housing in the grounds of Digby Mental Hospital is Clyst Heath, and the words 'Lunatic Asylum' have been gouged off the foundation stone of the main building. The West of England Eye Infirmary has become the Hotel Barcelona, despite an Exonian's excellent suggestion that the name Peerless would not only suit a luxury hotel but also serve as a reminder of its original use.

Disdain for the commemoration of benefactors has also affected local schools. Bishop Blackall's Girls' School and Hele's School for boys were each named after their generous founders. They have been amalgamated and rechristened St Peter's High School. The names of Vincent Thompson and John Stocker, long-standing members of the city's Education Committee, have been dropped from the schools they nurtured.

All of Exeter's state and church schools underwent a major reorganisation in 1973. The secondary schools would henceforward cater only for 12- to 16-year-olds. A single sixth-form college would provide for the senior years. This was the old Tech which had taken over the original premises of Hele's School and become Exeter College. Twenty-five years later it was realised that it is better for children to make a start on secondary subjects at 11, and Exeter's schools will soon revert to this arrangement.

Exeter University has expanded greatly since it received its royal charter in 1956. Student numbers have risen to about 10,000, many from overseas.

98 View of the cathedral from Bedford Street preserved in the rebuilding of the 1960s.

99 University of Exeter, Streatham Campus, photographed by John Saunders in 1995, showing Northcote House tower, Library on left, Great Hall in centre and Northcott Theatre on right.

There is no longer a predominance of 'green wellies' from the Home Counties. The University continues its policy of providing halls of residence for about half of all students. People attending conferences enjoy the lovely green campus in the vacations. New buildings have spread steadily across the slopes of the Streatham Estate. The Northcott Theatre opened in 1967 to serve the city and the University. Next to it is the Great Hall, which accommodates concerts as well as examinations and degree ceremonies.

The University gave up its toehold in the city centre when its Gandy Street premises became the Arts Centre in 1983. However, it had joined forces with St Luke's Training College in 1978, and St Luke's has kept its own campus on Heavitree Road. Part of the new Peninsula Medical School is situated there, handy for the Royal Devon and Exeter Hospital for practical work. Exeter has had a postgraduate medical school since 1967, and a department of General Practice since 1973, and now has the undergraduate medical school that it had long hoped for.

The University is no longer an 'ivory tower'. It promotes strong links with local business. As everywhere, accountants influence its decisions. The philosophy department has been closed, and the photographic service, and the music department has recently been under threat. The areas of growth are Finance and Investment Studies and Leadership Training. Arab and Islamic Studies are important; they have a beautiful new Institute on the hillside between Reed Hall and Mardon. There are Innovation Centres allowing new hi-tech businesses to enjoy three years with the support of the University's facilities.

Hi-tech and internet businesses are becoming Exeter's major industries in the new millennium. Ten years ago many new office buildings stood empty. Since then, the city council, the business

100 The University College of the South West, Bradninch Place 1905-83, now the Phoenix Arts Centre, Gandy Street.

community and the University have joined forces to encourage relocation and economic growth. The Meteorological Office moved here in 2003 and employs 1,300; London Electricity opened large offices adjacent to them at Sowton soon after. Government departments moving out of London may also choose Exeter for its 'quality of life'.

The South West Regional Development Agency is based here, with responsibility for overseeing the economic growth of the entire peninsula. The Bank of England has opened an office to collect information on local business. There are moves to open a Science Park.

The latest figures show that about 25 per cent of the working population are employed in administration, health and education. Another 25 per cent work in distribution, hotels and restaurants, while 20 per cent are in banking, finance and insurance. Only 13 per cent of the city's workforce are still involved in manufacturing.

The civic status of the city has undergone several changes since 1960. In 1966 it annexed Pinhoe and the proudly independent town of Topsham. Local government reorganisation in 1974 made Exeter subject to Devon County Council. The city was no longer a separate county with its own sheriff. In the 1990s it bid unsuccessfully for unitary status. The Queen had at least allowed the city to retain the title of Mayor for the elected chairman of its Council. After all, Exeter was one of the earliest towns in England to have a mayor. In the Queen's jubilee year she upgraded the title to Lord Mayor.

Members of Parliament in the past forty years have alternated between Labour and Conservative, with a growing Liberal and Lib Dem vote. The Exeter constituency is now considered too large to be represented by one MP. How should it be split? Should it shed Topsham? Or cut adrift the area west of the river? The debate continues.

In 1960 Hoskins deplored the city's lack of culture and the council's philistinism. Since then, as he hoped, the expanding University has brought a range of benefits: academic families move in; creative students like it here so much that they stay on after graduating and set up drama companies, art displays and poetry groups. There are countless clubs, societies, discussion groups, choirs and local history societies. The Devon and Exeter Institution has taken on a new lease of life, staffed by volunteers. The Royal Albert Memorial Museum provides a lively programme of changing exhibitions, lunchtime lectures and children's activities. There are several small theatres in town, including one in the Phoenix Arts Centre, in addition to the Northcott on the Streatham Estate. The city council was wrong to characterise Exeter's culture in a recent survey as 'shopping and eating'. The city has much more to offer than that.

The new Crown Courts now under construction on Western Way will enable the buildings in Rougemont Castle to be vacated. Visitors will have access to the Castle Yard and the walk along the city walls. Tourism has become a major industry. The council runs annual festivals, opening and closing with firework displays. Redcoat Guides provide free tours. The city is now twinned with four others: Rennes, Bad Homburg, Yaroslavl and Terracina. It is proud of its heritage, the tangible survivals of two thousand years of history.

101 In October 2003 this plaque was put on W.G. Hoskins' birthplace, above his grandparents' bakery. He wrote of Exeter: 'I was born here, my family have lived here for a hundred and fifty years, and I can quote the Latin tag "This is my love, this is my country" [Virgil, *Aeneid* 4. 347]. This is where I belong. This is my own landscape.'

Exeter Street-names and Place-names

ALBERT STREET (Newtown) was built in the 1840s and named after the Prince Consort.

BARBICAN STEPS, so called from a *barbican* on the city walls at or near the Snail Tower.

BARING CRESCENT was named after Sir Thomas Baring, the ground landlord, who leased land for building here to Mr Brown, 'the projector of this extensive improvement to the city of Exeter'. The first stone was laid on 3 September 1818. Ten houses had been finished by 1828. 'Mr Brown' was probably John Brown, builder, of Holloway Street.

BARING PLACE was built by William Hooper from 1808 onwards. Twelve houses were originally planned but only four had been built by 1816. In 1816 Hooper received permission to build nine larger houses which would sell better. So called because the land belonged to Sir Thomas Baring.

BARLEY HOUSE (now the County Library) was originally called Barley Mount. Barley means 'barley clearing' and is first recorded in 1298. A house stood here long before the present one, which was built about 1800. The older house was garrisoned by Fairfax in the siege of Exeter in 1646 as it commanded a fine view of the city.

BARNFIELD CRESCENT was designed and built by Matthew Nosworthy (1750-1831). Only eight houses were built out of the 23 that were intended. It was apparently designed to be a 'circus' like Bedford Circus. Takes its name from the field between Southernhay and the Larkbeare Brook, which was called the Barn Field. In the 16th century it had been called St John's Fields. The Crescent was begun in 1792 but not completed for some years.

BARTHOLOMEW STREET was called *Britayne* for many centuries, being the area occupied by the British in Saxon times. On St Bartholomew's Day in 1637 (24 August) Bishop Hall opened a new cemetery, the original cemetery in the Cathedral Yard being full. This was called Bartholomew Yard (later it became the churchyard of Allhallows-on-the-Walls) and Bartholomew Street acquired its present name.

BEACON LANE leads towards Beacon Hill, the eminence above Pinhoe. On the summit was an old fire beacon, but it was probably a look-out place long before that as it covers a wide view of east Devon and looks right over the city of Exeter also.

BEAR STREET was named after the *Bear Inn*, town house of the abbots of Tavistock, which stood in South St. on the site of the present Roman Catholic church.

BEDFORD STREET takes its name from the Earl of Bedford, who in 1539 acquired the site of the house of the Black Friars (Dominicans) after its surrender to the king. On the site of the friary the earls of Bedford built Bedford House, which they used for a time as a town house. This gave way in 1773 to Bedford Circus, now destroyed.

BLACKBOY ROAD. So called after the *Black Boy*, a public house in the neighbourhood. The 'Black Boy Turnpike' is recorded in 1782.

BONHAY is not recorded before 1558 but must be older. A 'hay' is an enclosed piece of ground (cf. Shilhay). Bonhay may derive from the French *bon*, 'good', but the early forms of the name are lacking.

BOWHILL (in St Thomas) means 'curved hill'. First recorded in 1249, it was a seat of the Holland family, related to the Dukes of Exeter. The present house has a fine hall of 15th-century date, and other traces of the medieval mansion of the Hollands.

BRADNINCH PLACE belonged anciently to the Duchy of Cornwall. The head of the honour in Devon was Bradninch, hence this name. Bradninch Place was first built up early in the 17th century with a row of private houses.

BRIDGE STREET was constructed in 1778 as an avenue leading to the new Exe Bridge and so became the direct route out of the city on the west.

BROADGATE was the principal gate from the High Street into the Close, when the latter was walled round in 1286. It was demolished in 1825.

BULL MEADOW takes its name from an ancient inn *The Bull*, which stood on this side of Magdalen Street in the 17th century and earlier. The meadow was called after it.

BURY MEADOW is recorded in 1585 as 'Berry Mead'. The meaning of Berry is not clear but it probably relates to the earthwork (*burh*) near by at Danes Castle (q.v.). Bury Meadow was used as a burial ground for cholera victims in 1832 but the name is older than this and does not derive from this fact.

BUTCHER ROW was the name given to the top end of Smythen Street, occupied by a long row of butchers' stalls. It was called Butcher Row from the early 15th century onwards, but disappeared as a name in the late 19th century.

CASTLE STREET takes its name from the Norman castle at its head. The present Castle Street was cut in 1772, but the line of the original medieval street may be seen on the right as one goes up.

CATHERINE STREET is so called after St Katherine's Almshouses, founded by John Stevens, a canon of the cathedral, shortly before 1457. The little chapel still stands, amid the ruins of the almshouses (destroyed in 1942). Before the almshouses were built the street seems to have been called Doddehay Street—'Dodda's hay or enclosure'—Dodda being a Saxon owner of property on this site.

CHEEKE STREET was called after the Cheeke (or Chick) family who were substantial brewers, and later property owners, in St Sidwell's from Elizabethan times onwards. Cheeke Street was developed on some of their property in the early 19th century.

CHICHESTER PLACE, a fine colonnaded terrace in Southernhay, was built by William Hooper in 1824-5.

COLLETON CRESCENT is named after the Colleton family, several of whom were merchants in Exeter in the 16th and 17th centuries. They owned land all round here. Colleton Crescent was begun in 1802, the foundation stone of the centre house being laid by Miss Louisa Colleton on 3 September. The Crescent was completed in 1814.

COMBE STREET takes its name from the valley in which it lay, now largely filled up. It was originally an open steep-sided valley with a stream running down it, but a street had grown up here as early as 1256. It had an alternative name of Rock Lane taken from the chapel of St Roch which once stood here. Roch was always pronounced as Rock. St Roch is the special saint invoked against pestilence and skin diseases.

COUNTESS WEAR is named after the Countess of Devon who constructed a weir across the river Exe here in the year 1286.

COWICK STREET takes its name from the Saxon manor of Cowic which lay on this side of the river. The name means 'cow farm'. Later this part became generally known as St Thomas, from the dedication of the parish church (consecrated in 1412).

COWLEY BRIDGE is first recorded as a bridge in 1286, but is almost certainly on or near the Roman crossing of the river. Cowley means 'Cufa's clearing' in the woods that covered this piece of country in Saxon times.

CRICKLEPIT LANE led to Cricklepit Mills which were first built about 1180-90. The name was then *Crickenpette*, and probably means 'the pit or hollow beneath the cliffs'. The old Welsh word *Creic* means 'a rock, a cliff'. The city wall runs along the top of a low cliff here and Cricklepit lay directly beneath.

DANES CASTLE was actually a small earthen fortification, probably thrown up in 1136, when Exeter castle was under siege by King Stephen. It lay on the farther side of the deep Longbrook valley. In the 18th century it was wrongly attributed to the Danes and so got its present name. The earthwork was covered by a reservoir in 1834 but revealed again when the reservoir was moved in 1992.

DENMARK ROAD was cut from Magdalen Road to Paris St. in 1832 but not named until about 1863 when Edward, Prince of Wales, married Princess Alexandra of Denmark.

DIX'S FIELD was named after Mr Dix, who invited offers for a building lease, or outright purchase, in 1796. Eventually Matthew Nosworthy, an Exeter builder, put up houses on both sides of a small green about 1808. Largely destroyed in 1942.

DURYARD means 'deer fold'. [Alternatively it is the city's 'door-yard' or land outside the gate.—HMH] It was a hunting park of the Anglo-Saxon kings when they visited their royal city of Exeter, and was eventually given to the city, perhaps by King Athelstan about the year 930. It belonged to the city until the early 18th century when it was sold off. The main sales of land took place 1700-3. There are two good houses on this estate—Great Duryard, built by Sir Thomas Jefford about 1686-90, with later alterations and additions, and Duryard House, built about 1700, with some 19th-century additions.

EASTGATE takes its name from one of the four medieval gateways of the city.

EGYPT LANE disappeared in the rebuilding of the city after the Second World War. The name is an odd one. It occurs on Rocque's map of 1744 simply as Egypt and is probably not much older than that. The significance of the name is quite lost but it may be a slang term of some kind.

EWINGS LANE lay off Edmund St. Formerly called St Mary's Lane, from the fact that the church of St Mary Steps had property here. Called Ewan's

Lane or Ewings Lane after one Nicholas Ewens who held land here in the mid-16th century 'late enclosed between the Citie walls and the mill leat'. A remnant of this lane is now called Ewings Square.

EXE ISLAND was formed by the cutting of the main leat (that nearest the city walls), probably in the tenth century. It remained a marsh for some time, but by the 12th century was drained and being built up. The name is first recorded as 'insula Ex' about the middle of the 12th century. Exe Island became a separate manor, belonging to the earls of Devon until the downfall of the Courtenays in 1538. In 1550 the manor was given to the city by King Edward VI.

EXE STREET, formerly Exe Lane, is shown on Hooker's map of 1587. It ran down to the river at Bonhay Mills (now the *Mill on the Exe* pub).

EXWICK, now a village on the west side of the Exe, was a Saxon manor, held by Baldwin, the sheriff of Devon, in 1086. It means 'the dairy farm (wic) by the Exe'.

FAIRPARK ROAD was named after a field called Fair Park, because of its beautiful situation.

FORE STREET is a common street-name in Devon towns. It is always a continuation of a High Street (as at Totnes) and seems to mean 'the street before' or 'below' the main street.

FRIARS WALK is named after the Franciscan or Grey Friars who moved to this site in 1303. Their lands eventually came into the hands of the Colleton family who sold it off for building in 1829. All round this district are charming little villas and cottages of the 1830s and 1840s. Colleton Villa at the bottom of The Friars, in the Greek Revival style, is especially notable.

FRIERNHAY STREET led to 'the friars' enclosure' (hay), the plot of ground where the Franciscan friars had their original house until they moved to a new site outside the South Gate in 1303. The 'friars enclosure' is represented today by the enclosure of the former churchyard of Allhallows-on-the-Walls. From 1669 onwards the weekly market for horses was held here every Friday.

FROG STREET was formed when Exe Island was built up. Before that it was simply the swampy bank of the wider river Exe, frequented by frogs which gave their name to the new medieval street. The street has been widened to become a major part of the traffic system by the Exe Bridges.

GANDY STREET was called *Currestreet* originally. The exact meaning is not clear. It may mean 'dog street' from the number of these objectionable animals who frequented it (cf. Catte Street in Oxford), or it may derive from *curray*, 'currying of leather'—hence the street where the leather curriers carried on their trade. This is the more likely meaning. By the early 18th century the name had changed to Gandy Lane after the family of that name who had a large house and other property here.

GERVASE AVENUE is a modern road named after the Nicholas and Walter Gervase who between them were largely responsible for the building of the first stone bridge over the Exe.

GLASSHOUSE LANE derives its name from the glass factory which was established by the river in the late 17th century.

GOLDSMITH STREET was so called in the 13th century from the goldsmiths who worked here. Whether it had an earlier name is not certain, but there is a 'lost' street-name, Corn Street, recorded in 1236 and apparently superseded not long afterwards. Possibly this was the earlier name of Goldsmith Street.

GUINEA STREET is so called as far back as the time of Henry II. It may derive from the old dialect word *ginnel*, still used in some parts of the country for a narrow passage. The earliest spelling is *Genne street*.

HALDON, though not strictly an Exeter name (except in the modern Haldon Rd.) is so much a part of nearly every Exeter view that some mention is called for. This beautiful range of hills, several miles long, closes the entire western horizon. To derive its name, as do the editors of *The Place-Names of Devon*, from the Old English word *hagol*, meaning 'hail', is the purest academic nonsense. Why should a whole range of hills be permanently named after some hailstorm, however remarkable? The difficulty arises because the name is not recorded before 1281, too late for satisfactory early forms, but two reasonable suggestions may be made. The name may be derived from the Old English *Haw-hyll dun*, meaning 'look-out hill', *dun* being the down or common pasture along the whole range. The look-out would probably have been on what is now Telegraph Hill, which was anciently called Warborough Hill. Warborough derives from *weard beorg*, meaning 'the hill from which a watch was kept'. Polwhele says there was formerly a beacon here, and the hill commands a magnificent view of the Exe estuary and east Devon. There was almost certainly another ancient look-out on Pen Hill (now called Haldon Belvedere) which commands an even more sweeping view in all directions. Haldon would have been an incomparable outer defence for Roman Isca and Saxon Exeter. Alternatively, the name may come from the Old English word *halig*, meaning 'holy'. So it would mean 'the holy hill', presumably of some pre-Christian religion, rather like *nimet*, the British name for a considerable district in mid-Devon, which means 'a shrine, a holy place'.

HAMLIN LANE is called after the 16th-century merchant family of Hamlyn who presumably had property here. There is also a Hamlyns Lane in Exwick, named after the same family.

HEAVITREE was named after some ancient tree—either 'Hefa's tree' or perhaps *heafod treow*, 'the head, or chief, tree'. Though not recorded as a name before 1086, a Christian church has probably stood on this site since the seventh century. The tree must have had some special significance, perhaps religious.

HIGH STREET, the principal street of the city, has been in use for more than two thousand years, being part of a ridge-way of Iron-Age date.

HILLS COURT, at the foot of Pennsylvania, was formerly a hamlet of 'several genteel houses with good gardens, in a pleasant retired situation, free from the noise and smoke of the city' (Jenkins, 1806). It took its name from Sir John Hill, a medieval Lord Chief Justice who had his mansion here. All trace of this disappeared long ago.

HOLLOWAY STREET was originally called Carterne street (1291), the street where the carters lived. It changed its name in the 15th century to *Holoway*, so called because it descended into the steep hollow of the Larkbeare Brook between high-banked sides.

HOOPERN is first recorded as a name in 1225. It is a difficult name, and may mean 'the place where barrel-hoops were made'.

HOWELL ROAD, partly built up in the 1840s, is a modern name. The ancient name for centuries was Red Lane, from the colour of the exposed soil.

IRON BRIDGE was built across the valley of the Long Brook to avoid the steep descent and ascent of the old road (now Lower North Street). Completed in December 1835.

JAMES STREET was named after King James II, whose Declaration of Indulgence (1687) marked the end of enforcing conformity to the Church of England by law. In Exeter the Presbyterians erected a meeting-house in this street which was called James's Meeting in honour of the king. This meeting-house went out of use when George's Meeting was built in 1760. The old name of the street (before James St.) remains unknown.

KING STREET was cut through from Fore St. in 1834 and named after King William IV in the following year.

LAMB ALLEY is the name of a courtyard leading off the Close. It formerly ran through to the High Street where No. 45 High Street now stands but was stopped up when that house was built (probably in the 16th century). Possibly takes its name from an old inn of which there is now no record.

LARKBEARE means 'lark wood'. The deep valley here (at the foot of Holloway Street) was once wooded and noted for its larks. A house was built here in the 13th century (where Roberts Rd. now is) and was partly pulled down in 1889.

LITTLE SILVER is shown (though not named) on Rocque's map of 1744. No satisfactory explanation of the name, which occurs in several places in Devon, has ever been given.

LIVERYDOLE has nothing to do with the doling out of liveries. A *dole* is a piece of land, in this case the triangular piece enclosed by three ancient roads. The first part of the name probably derives from the Old English personal name *Leofhere*, the name of a former owner. Hence 'Leofhere's piece of land'.

LONGBROOK STREET took its name from the stream that flowed across the foot of the street. The street itself began to be built up in the 12th and 13th centuries. It was also a Roman road, leading from the East Gate of the city up to the signal station on the top of Pennsylvania.

LUDWELL LANE is named after an ancient spring Ludwell, 'the loud spring', probably because it bubbled audibly out of the ground.

MADDOCKS ROW was cut through the city wall from Paul Street in 1772. Named after a local landlord or builder who put up a row of pleasant little houses here.

MAGDALEN STREET is first recorded in 1419 as *Maudeleynestrete*, so the original pronunciation was Maudlin (as at Oxford). Named after the leper hospital of St Mary Magdalen which stood well out of the city on this side since early times. It is recorded as 'the street of St Mary Magdalene' about 1259, so it was built up by the early 13th century.

MARKET STREET only goes back to 1835 when the Lower Market was built. The architect was Charles Fowler, an Exeter man, who built much elsewhere.

MARY ARCHES STREET is recorded about 1260 and takes its name from St Mary Arches church.

MARYPOLE HEAD was the original name for the hill now known as Pennsylvania (see later). The name is not recorded before 1461, too late for a satisfactory explanation, but it clearly relates to a pool. It may be 'boundary pool' from the old word *mere* meaning 'a boundary'. But it may equally be 'Mary pool', a holy spring bubbling into a pool. The exact site was probably on the right-hand side of the road leading down to Stoke Canon (on the old city boundary), where a spring called 'brides' spring' flowed in ancient times. The 'brides' spring' is named in a land-charter of 938 and pretty certainly refers to a spring associated with fertility rites for young brides in pre-Christian times. In later centuries the spring or pool became associated with the Virgin Mary. This ancient spring now rises in the field just below the left-hand side of the road, having been cut by the present road.

MATFORD LANE takes its name from the old house Matford, itself a corruption of *Madeworthy* and nothing to do with the Matford on the other side of the river. The present very attractive house was built about 1600, but an earlier house stood here as *Madaworthi* is referred to as early as *c.*1250. It was 'Mada's farm'. The existing house was built by Sir George Smyth who was mayor of Exeter in 1586, 1597, and 1607.

MELBOURNE STREET (and PLACE), named after the Lord Melbourne who was Prime Minister 1835-41 when this part was being developed for building. There are some pleasant houses of this date round here.

MILK STREET is first recorded in the reign of Henry II but was undoubtedly older. It was 'the street of the milk-sellers' who also had their cow-sheds here.

MINCINGLAKE ROAD, a modern road, takes its name from *Mincinglake* which means 'the nuns' stream'. It flowed past St Katherine's priory (for nuns) and so got its name, but the ancient name was almost certainly the Wonford (see later).

MINT LANE runs through the former cloister of St Nicholas Priory. The name was first used in the 18th century, referring either to a Civil War Royalist mint in St Olave's parish or to a mint in Mary Arches Street set up for William III's recoinage of 1696.

MOUNT RADFORD was originally called Radford after the Laurence Radford who built a house in this commanding position (where Barnardo Rd. now is) about 1570. This house was known as Radford Place. The house and surroundings were fortified in the Civil War and, like many other such fortified sites, came to be called Mount (cf. Mount Boone at Dartmouth or Mount Wise at Plymouth). Mount Radford gave its name to a whole district when it was developed *c.*1830-50.

MUSGRAVES ALLEY (destroyed in 1942) led off High Street nearly opposite Bedford St. to a large house which stood in its own grounds, known as Musgrave House. This was formerly the home of Dr William Musgrave (1655-1721), a learned physician and antiquary, who practised at Exeter. He was secretary of the Royal Society in 1685. Settled in Exeter in 1691 and practised with great success here for thirty years. He is buried in St Leonard's churchyard. His house was demolished in 1878.

NEW BUILDINGS (Gandy St.) are so called on John Rocque's map of 1744.

NEWTOWN was the name given to a large district on the south side of Sidwell Street which was developed for working-class houses in the second quarter of the 19th century. Much of this area was destroyed in the air raid of 1942 but has been redeveloped and regenerated as a community.

NORTH STREET was originally Northgate St. The meaning is obvious. It was probably the Roman road out of the city to the north, over St David's Hill and so to the crossing of the Exe at or near Cowley Bridge.

NORTHERNHAY—*hay* simply means 'enclosure', and this was the enclosed area on the northern side of the city corresponding with Southern-hay on the other side. The name is first recorded about 1415. In 1612 it was laid out as a pleasure-walk for citizens and has remained so ever since.

OLD TIVERTON ROAD was the main road to Tiverton, over Stoke Hill, before the present road beside the river was cut from Cowley Bridge to Stoke Canon bridge in the early 19th century. Old Tiverton Road is a Roman road, and before that was an Iron-Age ridgeway, so it has been in use for some twenty to twenty-five centuries.

PALACE GATE was one of the medieval gateways into the Close, named after the adjacent palace of the bishops of Exeter.

PANCRAS LANE takes its name from the church of St Pancras here, now a pedestrian square in the Guildhall Shopping Precinct. It is a frequent habit in Exeter to drop the 'Saint', as in Sidwell Street, Paul Street, Martins Lane, and so on. It is a habit of very long standing as Paul Street is so called as early as 1240.

PARIS STREET is not recorded as a name until 1422. The meaning is uncertain. It may derive from the word *pearr*, 'an enclosure', but if so the significance of this is not obvious. In the 13th century it was called Shitbrook Street, from the name of the stream (now buried and used as a storm sewer) that flowed across the bottom of the street at what is now called the Triangle.

PARLIAMENT STREET is the narrowest street in Exeter. Although ancient (it is a medieval lane between High St. and Waterbeer St.), its name is comparatively modern, bestowed about 1832 when the Reform Bill put Parliament in the news. The precise point of the name is not clear: perhaps it is an obscure joke. In 1836 the inhabitants of Waterbeer St. petitioned to have Parliament St. widened, and subscribed £130 for the purpose, but nothing was done and the 'street' remains one of the narrowest in England.

PAUL STREET named after the church of St Paul. The medieval church was replaced by a delightful little late 17th-century building, but this was wantonly destroyed in 1936. The then bishop (Cecil) authorised this vandalism, and the site was occupied by an emergency water tank (for war purposes), later by a prefabricated structure.

PENNSYLVANIA originated with the building of four houses at Pennsylvania Terrace (now P. Park) in 1822-3 by Mr Joseph Sparkes, a partner in the General Bank. Mr Rowe of Paris Street was the builder. Mr Sparkes, who financed the building, was a member of the Society of Friends, and adopted the name Pennsylvania for his new terrace from the province established by William Penn in the U.S.A. During the middle decades of the 19th century the name was extended to cover the whole district.

POLSLOE ROAD, though relatively modern as a built-up area, runs along the top of a ridge with fine views across Exeter and was used as a ridgeway in the Iron Age. It takes its name from Polsloe Priory, some distance away. Polsloe is an old name, being recorded in Domesday Book. It means 'Poll's marsh', Poll being some Saxon owner of the low-lying ground beside the Wonford stream where the priory was later built.

PRESTON STREET was 'the street of the priests' as early as the time of Henry II (*c*.1160). Exeter was full of churches and chapels—over thirty at this date—but there were no rectory or vicarage houses because there were no parishes as we understand the word. Therefore the priests lived in a colony like many other occupations.

QUARRY LANE is called after the large quarries of Heavitree stone which were first opened up in the 15th century. Most of the Exeter parish churches are built of this stone and it appears in many other buildings. Quarry Lane was a Roman road, leading straight down to the stream-crossing at Wonford (see later under that name).

QUAY LANE leads straight down to the old Quay. It is probably on the line of a Roman road from the quay of that time up to the South Gate.

QUEEN STREET is named after Queen Victoria, though it was actually begun in March 1835. The statue of Queen Victoria near the High St. end was erected on 24 May 1848, the Queen's birthday. This was an entirely new street crossing the Longbrook valley and was called Higher Market Street at first.

RACK STREET occurs as Racke Lane in 1562 because racks, or frames for drying cloths, were set up near here. Earlier, in the 12th century it had another name—Tyght Street, the meaning of which is obscure. It may derive simply from the old word *thite*, meaning 'close, compact', a reference to its narrowness.

RED COW was the name of an inn in the 17th century. The inn has closed but the locality retains the name.

RICHMOND ROAD was built up in the mid-19th century and later. It was formerly called Pound Lane because the cattle-pound of the manor of Duryard stood on the corner of this lane (on the site of No. 24, St David's Hill).

RIFFORD ROAD is modern, but Rifford is a very old name. Adam de Rifford, who was mayor of Exeter 1246-54, must have had a considerable house here. Probably the name means 'rye ford', a ford over the Wonford brook near which rye was grown.

RINGSWELL AVENUE, a modern road but an old name. *Ringeswille* is recorded in 1269, and means 'Hring's spring', Hring being the name of a former owner of the land here.

ROSEBARN LANE was originally Rowe's Barn Lane, a self-explanatory name. Rowe was the name of an Exeter butcher, who leased the fields here and erected a barn about the year 1700.

ROUGEMONT means 'the red hill', so called from the colour of the volcanic rock of which it is formed. The castle was begun in 1068 and was known as Exeter Castle. The earliest reference to 'the red hill' is in a Dean and Chapter deed of about 1250, which is a grant of land *super rubeum montem*. William of Worcester, about 1478, says it was then called *Rougemont*, and the name has stuck to it ever since.

RYDON LANE is a very old road. It formed part of the boundary of Topsham in 937 when King Athelstan gave the manor to St Mary's abbey at Exeter. It was then called simply 'the way'. The name means 'rye hill' probably because this rising ground grew excellent rye. Sandy Park, near the lane, suggests the kind of soil that suited rye.

ST DAVID'S HILL is called after the church of St David. It is a Roman road in origin, leading from the north gate of the city to somewhere in mid-Devon.

ST LEONARD'S ROAD was formerly the carriage-drive leading to Mount Radford House from Magdalen Road. It was developed for building in 1830-2 and at first called Higher Terrace and Lower Terrace.

ST MARTIN'S LANE, named from St Martin's church, to which it leads. The church was consecrated in 1065, and the street is probably at least as old as that.

SHILHAY is recorded as The Shellye on the Exeter map of 1587. *Hay* is an enclosed piece of ground. The prefix here may mean 'a shelf or a ledge', probably 'an enclosed shelf of ground jutting into the river'.

SHOOTING MARSH STILE as a name is a relic of the days when there was good shooting along the banks of the Exe here.

SIDWELL STREET takes its name from the church of St Sidwell. It began to be built up, just outside the East Gate of the city, during the 12th century.

SMYTHEN STREET is first recorded as a street-name in the time of Henry II (mid-12th century). It was 'the street of the smiths' who must have been numerous in early medieval Exeter, probably making mostly armour and horse trappings.

SNAIL TOWER is the name given to the angle of the city walls near All-hallows churchyard. A tower is recorded here in 1348 and 1437 (city records), probably named 'snail' after its colour and perhaps odd shape.

SOUTH STREET, often called Southgate Street in the earliest civic records, has been built up since Saxon times at least. The derivation of the name is obvious.

SOUTHERNHAY was the *Hay* or enclosure on the south side of the city as opposed to Northernhay. It was already so called in 1265. The present Southernhay Green, one of the most attractive features of any town in England, marks the line of the great town ditch outside the walls, formerly known as *Crulditch*. This name derives from the medieval word *crull*, meaning 'curly', from the curved or curling line of the ditch on this side of the city.

SPICER ROAD, a late Victorian road which derives its name from the ancient Exeter family of Spicer who had property here. They lived in Exeter from the early 13th century (at least) until the early 19th, their name being derived of course from their original trade, that of a dealer in spices.

STEPCOTE HILL, one of the most interesting survivals in Exeter. It is the original main street of the medieval city, with steps at each side for pedestrians and a narrow cobbled roadway for pack-horses. The name, however, probably derives from the Old English word *stype*, for 'steep', rather than from the steps. It would mean 'the steep street'.

STREATHAM HALL (now Reed Hall) was built in the Italianate villa style in 1867 by Richard Thornton West, a retired East India merchant. At his death in 1878 he was a millionaire, the only one ever to reside in Exeter.

SUN STREET ran from South Street to Preston Street. It took its name from the *Sun Inn*, which stood on the N.W. side of the street. The *Sun Inn* existed in the 1690s, at which date the street was called Billeter Lane. The meaning of Billeter is uncertain but it may derive from *billet*, 'a note'—hence 'writers' lane'—where the medieval scriveners congregated. Destroyed in 1942.

TADDIFORD is recorded as a name as early as 1280. It was 'the toad-frequented ford', and was the ford by which the Roman road over St David's Hill crossed the stream that flowed down the Hoopern Valley (now called Taddiford Brook) near the *Red Cow Inn*.

TRICHAY STREET was the original name of the medieval street that ran from Pancras Lane, parallel with Waterbeer Street, towards North Street. This street was blocked up in 1349 by the building of the rectory-house of St Kerrians. It was one of the numerous *hays* of medieval Exeter (an enclosure of some kind) but the meaning of the prefix is quite unknown. It may be a personal name, similar to Doddehay Street (the old name of Catherine Street) which was so called after one Dodda. The name has been transferred to a pedestrian way in the Guildhall Shopping Precinct running from the High Street at right angles to its historic direction.

UNION ROAD was formerly called Pester Lane, but the name Union Road was given in 1835 to the route running all the way from Pennsylvania Road to the Union Workhouse below Polsloe Road.

VELWELL ROAD, a modern road named after an old spring that flowed here, recorded in 13th-century deeds. It was *fealu-wielle*, 'the pale brown spring' from the peculiar colour of its water.

WATERBEER STREET is so called as early as 1253, but there is no doubt that it is Saxon in origin, if not Roman. The meaning of the name is obscure. The likeliest origin is 'the street of the water bearers', another medieval street devoted to a particular trade or occupation.

WEIRFIELD ROAD is named after the Weir Field, which itself derived its name from Trew's Weir or St Leonard's Weir, constructed in 1564.

WELL STREET is named after an ancient spring, possibly the holy spring of St Sidwell which broke out of the ground behind St Sidwell's church, if not directly underneath it.

WEST STREET led to the old West Gate of the city.

WHIPTON formerly a village outside Exeter but now absorbed into the city. It was called after a Saxon owner, Wippa—hence 'Wippa's farm'.

WONFORD is an ancient name and one that is difficult to explain. Though later an insignificant place, and now embedded in the populous district of Heavitree, it was in Saxon times the head of a large royal estate dating from the middle of the seventh century, and the head of the hundred of Wonford. The hundred court probably met 'at the chief tree' (*heafod treow*, now Heavitree), an elevated site in Heavitree churchyard itself, which commands a fine view. This site had the additional advantage of being within a few yards of the principal Roman road into Exeter, and also of the ancient ridge-way along Mount Pleasant and Polsloe Road.

The name Wonford was taken from the stream (now called Mincinglake in its upper reaches) which rises on the southern slopes of Stoke Hill and reaches the Exe at what used to be called Northbrook Park. The earliest written record of the stream-name is *wynford* in a Saxon charter of 937, and is very likely to be a British (Celtic) name meaning 'the fair stream' from the Welsh words *gwyn* meaning 'white, fair, or holy' and *ffrwd*, meaning 'a stream'. This would suit the appearance of the Wonford which once flowed (and still does in places) through the most beautiful pastoral scenery.

Another possibility is that the prefix derives from the Old English word (*ge*)*winn*, meaning 'a fight, conflict'. So Wonford, if it is an English name rather than British, may mean 'battle ford', the scene of some ancient battle of which we now have no record. As the chief Roman road into Exeter crossed the stream at Wonford, just south of the present Heavitree Bridge, it may well have been the scene of a decisive battle.

Since river-names tend, however, so often to be Celtic in origin (like Exe, Clyst, Culm, and Creedy, all around Exeter) I incline to the view that Wonford is a Celtic stream-name meaning 'the fair stream' or even perhaps 'the holy stream'. In what connection it may have been holy we do not know, but for a similar name see under *Haldon*.

WREFORDS LANE is probably named after William Wreyford who farmed Barton Place in the early 19th century. It is an ancient road, running from Marypole Head down to the river-crossing at Cowley Bridge, so it must have had an earlier name than this.

Suggestions for Further Reading

Allan, J.P., *Exeter Guildhall* (1991); *Exeter's Underground Passages* (1994); *St Nicholas Priory Exeter* (1999). Useful booklets published by Exeter City Council.

Allan, J.P., Henderson, C.G. and Higham, R.A., 'Saxon Exeter' in J. Haslam (ed.), *Anglo-Saxon Towns in Southern England* (Chichester 1984)

Andriette, Eugene A., *Devon and Exeter in the Civil War* (Newton Abbot 1971)

Barlow, Frank (ed.), *Exeter and its Region*. A survey prepared for the meeting of the British Association in Exeter in 1969. Sections on the physical background, biology, archaeology, history, literature, economy and politics of the South-West, and aspects of the city of Exeter.

Barlow, Frank, Kathleen Dexter, Audrey Erskine and L.J. Lloyd, *Leofric of Exeter* (Exeter 1972). Essays commemorating the founding of Exeter Cathedral Library in 1072.

Bidwell, P.T.B., *Roman Exeter, Fortress and Town* (Exeter 1980)

Bradbeer, Doris M., *Joyful Schooldays* (Exeter 1973). A comprehensive history of the Exeter grammar schools: St John's Hospital, Exeter School, the Maynard, Hele's and Bishop Blackall.

Brockett, A., *Nonconformity in Exeter 1650-1875* (Manchester 1962)

Cherry, Bridget and Pevsner, Nikolaus, *Devon*, in *The Buildings of England* series (2nd edn, revised, Harmondsworth [Penguin Books] 1989); dedicated to W.G. Hoskins, pp. 358-441 on Exeter buildings, architecture and street-scenes.

Clapp, B.W., *The University of Exeter, a History* (University of Exeter 1982). From its beginnings in 1855 via its charter of 1955 to 1982.

Clark, E.A.G., *The Ports of the Exe Estuary, 1660-1860* (Exeter 1960). Relating the rise and decline of the port of Exeter to its geographical setting.

Clew, K.R., *The Exeter Canal* (Chichester 1984)

Conner, Patrick W., *Anglo-Saxon Exeter: a tenth-century cultural history* (Woodbridge, Suffolk, etc. 1993). Argues that the Exeter Book and other important Anglo-Saxon MSS were written in the scriptorium at Exeter.

Delderfield, Eric H., *Cavalcade by Candlelight: the story of Exeter's five theatres 1735-1950* (Exmouth 1950)

Erskine, Audrey (ed.), *The Fabric Rolls of Exeter Cathedral*, 2 vols (Exeter 1981-2). Documentary evidence for the building work.

Erskine, Audrey, Hope, V., and Lloyd, L.J., *Exeter Cathedral: a short history with description* (2nd edn, Exeter 1988)

Falla, Trevor, *Discovering Exeter: Heavitree* (Exeter Civic Society, 1983). One of a series inspired by W.G. Hoskins. Guided walks pin events to their locations.

Fox, Aileen, *Roman Exeter (Isca Dumnoniorum): excavations in the war-damaged areas 1945-7* (Manchester 1952). Excavations found signs of a forum and public bath, and a piece of 4th-c. pottery marked with the Christian chi-rho sign, but no evidence of a military fortress.

Fox, Aileen, *South-West England 300 BC-AD 600* (2nd edn, Newton Abbot 1973)

Gray, Todd, *Exeter Engraved*, 2 vols: *I: The secular city II: The cathedral, churches, chapels and priories* (Mint Press, Exeter, 2000, 2001). Reproduces engravings of Exeter buildings, landscpes and events.

Gray, Todd, *The Travellers' Tales: vol.I: Exeter* (Mint Press, Exeter 2000). Collects reports of visits to the city in diaries ranging from John Leland in 1542 to Margaret Halsey in 1937.

Greenaway, G.W., *Saint Boniface: three biographical studies* (London 1955). Commemorates the 12th-centenary festival of Boniface's martyrdom.

Greenaway, Joyce, *Discovering Exeter: St David's* (Exeter Civic Society 1981)

Harvey, Hazel, *Discovering Exeter: Pennsylvania* (1984); *Sidwell Street* (1986); *West of the River* (1989) (Exeter Civic Society)

Harvey, Hazel, *Exeter Past* (Chichester 1996). 2000 years of Exeter's history with illustrations.

Harvey, Hazel, *A Better Provision: the Royal Devon and Exeter Hospital 1948-1998* (Exeter 1998). Fifty years of the National Health Service.

Henderson, C.G., 'Exeter *(Isca Dumnoniorum)*' in G. Webster (ed.), *Fortress into City: the consolidation of Roman Britain, first century AD* (London 1988), 91-119

Henderson, C.G., 'The archaeology of Exeter Quay' in *Devon Archaeology* 4 (1991) 1-15

Henderson, C.G. and Bidwell, P., 'The Saxon Minster at Exeter' in S.M. Pearce (ed.), *The Early Church in Western Britain and Ireland* (Oxford 1982), 145-75

Holbrook, N. and Bidwell, P.D., *Roman Finds from Exeter* (Exeter 1991)

Hoskins, W.G., *Industry, Trade and People in Exeter 1688-1800* (Manchester 1935, reprinted Exeter 1968)

Hoyos-Saavedra, Eduardo, *Discovering Exeter: Twentieth-century Architecture* (Exeter Civic Society 2001)

Kain, Roger and Ravenhill, William (eds.), *Historical Atlas of South-West England* (Univ. of Exeter Press 1999). Includes C.G. Henderson, 'The city of Exeter from AD 50 to the early nineteenth century', pp. 482-98; Nicholas Orme and C.G. Henderson, 'Exeter Cathedral', 499-502; Richard Oliver, 'Map evidence of the growth of Exeter during the nineteenth century', 503-11; Andrew Gilg, 'Exeter in the twentieth century', 512-13.

Kelly, Francis (ed.), *Medieval Art and Architecture at Exeter Cathedral* (1991) – The British Archaeological Association Conference Transactions for the year 1985. The seventeen articles include discussions of the cathedral's archives, stones, misericords and polychromy.

Kowaleski, Maryanne, *Local Markets and Regional Trade in Medieval Exeter* (Cambridge 1995). Trading in Exeter around 1400.

MacCaffrey, W.T., *Exeter 1540-1640: the growth of an English county town.* (Cambridge, Mass. and London 1958). A study of the urban community.

Maggs, Colin, *Rail Centres: Exeter* (Ian Allan Ltd 1985). History of the stations and companies serving Exeter from 1844.

Meller, Hugh, *Exeter Architecture* (Chichester 1989). Photographs and descriptions of over 100 Exeter buildings in alphabetical order.

Minchinton, Walter, *Life to the City: an illustrated history of Exeter's water supply from the Romans to the present day* (Exeter 1987)

Newton, R., *Eighteenth-century Exeter* (Univ. of Exeter 1984). Covers 1688-1834, drawing on the Chamber Acts Books and newspapers of the time.

Newton, R., *Victorian Exeter* (Leicester Univ. Press 1968) Covers the politics, economy and development of the city 1837-1914.

Orme, Nicholas, *Education in the West of England 1066-1548* (Univ. of Exeter 1976). Details of the education supplied by Exeter's cathedral, friaries and other early schools.

Orme, Nicholas, *Exeter Cathedral As It Was 1050-1550* (Exeter 1986). The changing liturgy.

Orme, Nicholas, *The Cap and the Sword: Exeter and the rebellions of 1497* (Exeter City Council 1997)

Orme, Nicholas (ed.), *Unity and Variety: a history of the Church in Devon and Cornwall* (Exeter 1991)

Orme, Nicholas and Lepine, David, *Death and Memory in Medieval Exeter* (Devon and Cornwall Record Society 2003)

Passmore, Dick, *The Story of the Theatre Royal, Exeter* (Exeter, Mint Press 2002). The story until the theatre closed in 1962.

Pearce, S.M., *The Kingdom of Dumnonia* (Padstow 1978)

Pearce, S.M., *The Archaeology of South West Britain* (London 1981)

Pevsner, N. *see* Cherry, Bridget

Portman, D., *Exeter Houses 1400-1700* (University of Exeter 1966). A detailed illustrated study of the city's medieval domestic buildings, some since demolished.

Richardson, A.E. and Gill, C.L., *Regional Architecture in the West of England* (London 1924)

Roots, Ivan, *The Great Rebellion 1642-60* (Batsford 1966)

Roots, Ivan (ed.), *The Monmouth Rising* (Devon Books 1986). Lectures commemorating the events of 1685.

Russell, P.M.G., *A History of the Exeter Hospitals 1170-1948* (Exeter 1948)

Shapter, Thomas, *The History of the Cholera in Exeter in 1832* (London 1849). With woodcuts by John Gendall showing street-scenes of 1832.

Sharp, Thomas, *Exeter Phoenix* (The Architectural Press, London, for Exeter City Council 1946)

Stephens, W.B., *Seventeenth-century Exeter: a study of industrial and commercial development, 1625-1688* (Exeter 1958)

Stoyle, Mark, *Loyalty and Locality* (Exeter 1994). Patterns of support for Parliament and the King in the city and the county.

Stoyle, Mark, *Circled with Stone: Exeter's city walls 1485-1660* (University of Exeter 2003)

Sturt, John, *Revolt in the West: the western rebellion of 1549* (Devon Books 1987)

Swanton, Michael (ed.), *Exeter Cathedral, a celebration* (Dean and Chapter of Exeter 1991). Twenty-seven chapters on the history, fabric, furnishings and changing use of the cathedral.

Thomas, Peter, *Exeter Burning* (Halsgrove, Tiverton 2003), reissued as *Fire on the Wind* (1992)

Thomas, Peter, *The Golden Years* (Devon Books/Halsgrove, Tiverton 2003). Over 300 photographs from the Isca Collection showing developments in Exeter 1940-80.

Thomas, Peter and Warren, Jacqueline, *Aspects of Exeter* (Plymouth 1980). Marks the 1,900th anniversary of the city's foundation. Photographs from the Isca Collection illustrate the loss of historic buildings. Authoritative commentaries by J. Warren.

Todd, Malcolm, *The South-West to AD 1000* (London 1987). The archaeology and early history of the South-West from the first appearance of man.

Venn, Gilbert, *Discovering Exeter: St Leonard's* (Exeter Civic Society 1982)

Venning, Norman, *Exeter, the Blitz and Rebirth of the City* (Exeter 1988)

Wiseman, T.P., 'Titus Flavius and the Indivisible Subject' (inaugural lecture, Univ. of Exeter 1978). Vespasian's campaigns with the Second Legion across the south of Britain as far as Exeter.

Worrall, Geoff, *Target Exeter* (Exeter 1979). Pictures and memories of the 1942 Blitz.

Youings, Joyce, *Tuckers Hall, Exeter: the history of a provincial city company through five centuries* (Exeter 1968)

Index

Figures in **bold** type refer to illustrations.

EXETER IN 1960

PRINCIPAL PLACES OF INTEREST

1. Cathedral
2. Bishop's Palace
3. Deanery
4. Guildhall and *Turk's Head Hotel* (medieval inn)
5. Castle
6. Castle Gate House
7. St David's Church
8. Castle Moat
9. Entrance to Underground Passages
10. St Mary Arches Church
11. St Mary Steps Church
12. St Edmund's Church (for medieval bridge)
13. St Martin's Church
14. St Michael's Church
15. George's Chapel
16. St Nicholas Priory
17. Wynyard's Almshouses
18. Tuckers' Hall
19. Devon and Exeter Hospital (1741)
20. Custom House
21. Bonded Warehouses
22. Devon and Exeter Institution (formerly the town house of the Courtenays)
23. Law Library
24. Higher Market (1838)
25. *Royal Clarence Hotel*
26. 'Tudor House'
27. The Close (No. 10)
28. Medieval house (West Street)
29. Mol's Coffee House
30. High Street (Nos. 39-46)
31. South Street (No. 67)
32. Barnfield Crescent
33. Colleton Crescent
34. Rougemont House
35. Line of Medieval Exe Bridge (12th century)
36. Old Match Factory
37. Elizabethan Merchant's House (1567), next to Stuart Merchant's House
38. St Olave's Church
39. Holy Trinity Church
40. St Pancras Church
41. St Sidwell's Church
42. St Petrock's Church
43. Jewish Synagogue (1764)
44. Houses (18th-century)
45. *White Hart Hotel* (medieval and later)
46. St Stephen's Church
47. St Katherine's Almshouses and Chapel (medieval: ruined)
48. No. 5 The Close (medieval)
49. Wesleyan Chapel (1846)
50. Medieval Merchant's House (16 Edmund Street)
51. Colleton Villa (c.1830)
52. Wharfinger's Office (1778)

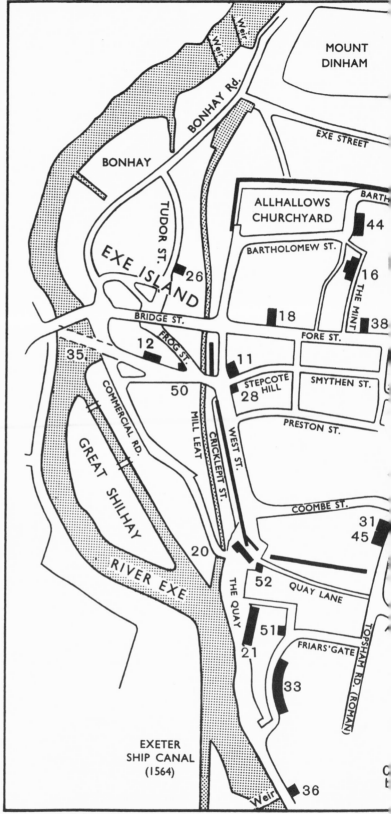

Based upon the Ordnance Survey Map, with the sanction of the Controller of H.M. Stationer